LETTING THE OUTSIDE IN
developing teaching and learning
beyond the early years classroom

A4 771

LETTING THE OUTSIDE IN
developing teaching and learning beyond the early years classroom

Edited by Rebecca Austin

Trentham Books

Stoke on Trent, UK and Sterling, USA

Trentham Books Limited
Westview House   22883 Quicksilver Drive
734 London Road   Sterling
Oakhill   VA 20166-2012
Stoke on Trent   USA
Staffordshire
England ST4 5NP

First published 2007. Reprinted 2008.

British Library Cataloguing-in-Publication Data
A catalogue record for this book is available from the British Library

ISBN: 978 1 85856 391 6

Cover photograph: Diane Wilkin

Designed and typeset by Trentham Print Design Ltd, Chester and
printed in Great Britain Cpod, Trowbridge, Wiltshire.

Contents

Acknowledgements • viii

Introduction • ix
Rebecca Austin

Chapter 1
Exploring the great outdoors • 1
Ian Shirley

Chapter 2
Taking the inside out • 13
Sue Hammond

Chapter 3
**Personal geographies – children and their
local environment** • 23
Terry Whyte

Chapter 4
**Using the built environment to generate
musical composition** • 33
Jonathan Barnes

Chapter 5
Inner city spaces • 53
Gina Donaldson

Chapter 6
Developing pedagogically appropriate practice • 63
Jane Williams-Siegfredsen

Chapter 7
'Making the best of what you've got': adopting and adapting
the Forest School approach • 75
Trisha Maynard

Chapter 8
Movement learning: bringing movement
into the classroom • 85
Richard Bailey and Ian Pickup

Chapter 9
Collect the Whole Set • 95
Gill Hope

Chapter 10
Children and their parents in schools:
a package deal • 107
Rebecca Austin

Chapter 11
The whole wide world: developing young children's
intercultural understanding • 117
Helen Taylor and Rebecca Austin

Chapter 12
Using without using up: involving teachers, children and
communities in sustainable lifestyles • 127
Alan Peacock

Notes on contributors • 137

References • 139

Index • 147

The school must represent present life – life as real and vital to the child as that which he carries on in the home, in the neighbourhood, or on the playground. (John Dewey, 1929)

Acknowledgements

Thank you to Steve for his unwavering support and encouragement and to Ellie and Ben for their patience.

Many thanks to all who have contributed to this book and also to Rosemary Walters.

Introduction

Rebecca Austin

The case against schools

Sunil, aged just four, is standing bemused in the Reception class while all the other children are sitting on the carpet, ready to listen. 'Where should you be?' asks the teaching assistant gently. 'At home,' comes the mournful reply. Sunil is described by his teacher as immature.

Pearl arrives in leafy Kent from a tough start in life in London's East End and, at the age of six, delights in subverting classroom practices. Today, one-by-one, she sends the other, obedient children who are well-versed in school behaviours, to read to the volunteer helper in the library – when no one is there. Pearl attends a social skills group at school.

Tony is enthusiastic and knowledgeable about the natural world and the local environment. His dad teaches him about the countryside around him on the frequent nature walks they take together when Tony, aged six, should be in school. Tony's reading and writing is not progressing and his teacher is concerned.

Lilly, a self-motivated five year old, arrives in school knowing exactly what she wants to learn and cannot understand why her teachers want her to learn something different. She is labelled 'difficult'.

I have no doubt that you have come across children like these, for whom the constraints of school and schooling seem to actively oppose their needs. These are the children for whom school does not do what it is supposed to do; these are the children who would learn best somewhere other than school. Good practitioners can make children's experiences of school better, but there is no denying that school does not meet the needs of all children all the time. How can it?

For most of us schools and schooling are firmly embedded within our own experiences. We have been told that education is the right of every child and have understood that this must be achieved, for the most part, through compulsory schooling. But schools are peculiar places:

> In one sense schools are curiously sequestered zones, with their spatial aloofness from the workaday and domestic environments, their routine exclusion of 'outsiders', their suspension of the ordinary rhythms of experience, their adherence to a strict timetable, their paraphernalia of uniforms and other rituals that lend them a strange continuity with an ancient academy, not to say a medieval monastery. (Dunne, 1995 p146-147)

Schools are appointed by society as the place where children are to be educated. But there are alternatives to schools – it is simply that many cultures have by and large settled for schools as the means by which children are to be educated. Schools represent the meeting point of social constructions of childhood – what children are like and what they need – and social constructions of education – why, what and how children should learn and be taught. What they are like is influenced by political, societal, financial and ideological pressures from a variety of sources: parents, governments, educationalists and more, and across the world and within a range of cultures, schools have evolved or not with similarities and differences in both policies and practices (see Alexander, 2000).

But whatever schools are like, there is no reason why they should be regarded as the best places for children to learn. All children, no matter where they live, learn outside school, in the years before they start formal schooling and in the many hours they spend at home and elsewhere. What they learn and how they learn it may be different, but they are learning nevertheless. There are many complex arguments about the nature and purpose of education (see Carr, 2005; McCulloch, 2005, Ball, 2004) and in England and elsewhere there are currently debates about the future of schooling (see TDA, 2006; Richards and Taylor, 1998; Hicks, 2002; Clark, 2005) in the light of changing technology and the perceived needs of society, alongside the issues raised by *Every Child Matters* (DfES, 2004). Arguments and discussions will continue to surface and re-surface in education, but the essence of education is ultimately manifested in classrooms and settings throughout the world by what happens within them. It is individual practitioners' interpretation of and responses to educational debates and government and school policies which determine the exact nature of the learning experiences of the children in their care. What you think about children, schools and education is fundamental to the kind of teacher you are and the learning experiences you therefore offer to the children with whom you work.

Schools remove children from their real world and offer them a constrained environment in which to learn which regularly fails to make connections with their experiences of what constitutes real life. Learning in school is often seen as something different from learning at home – and the two can seem to be mutually exclusive. There are many ways in which families are encouraged to make home more like school, but this book is about ways in which school can offer children more meaningful experiences within school by enabling them to connect learning in school with the wider world of their experiences: in the natural environment, at home and in the local community and beyond. Practitioners can aspire to create what Peter Woods describes as:

> ...a living classroom, with strong roots, continually evolving, which provides more of a link to children's own knowledge than an inside classroom, and a base for a holistic future, offering integration of curriculum and of self. (Woods, 1995, p63-64)

In the 1970s, Ivan Illich proposed the 'deschooling' of society (Illich, 1971), asserting that the things we have learned best we have learned outside of school and questioning the nature, role and purpose of schools in society. It seems unlikely that schools will disappear completely, but practitioners' understanding of the limitations of schools is essential if we are to develop practices which enable children to gain the most from their compulsory schooling.

The limitations of schools

How, then, are schools limited in what they have to offer? Throughout this book the contributing authors reiterate and develop principles for learning and teaching based on four basic ways in which schooling can restrict the learning experiences of the children who attend them – these are outlined below. This is not an exhaustive list and what is offered in this introduction is a starting point for consideration and deliberation – further reading is indicated where possible and is essential to develop a full understanding of the issues. Some of the limits referred to here are imposed by law, some by tradition and some by convenience – intentionally or not – but all are factors in the distancing of children's real life from their experiences in school.

The home/school divide

School and home are generally separated both physically and conceptually. Token gestures may be made towards the involvement of parents in their children's education, usually emphasising collaboration in school learning rather than making real efforts to build on home learning experiences. Children's enthusiasms and interests as well as their worries and fears about the world in which they live may only be included in controlled ways, either outside the curriculum – eg home visits, show and tell or within it – eg circle time, environmental education. This separation of home and school can set children at a distance from learning in school and require that they do the work in closing the gap and finding the connections between their real and school lives (see Crozier and Reay, 2005; Edwards, 2002).

School buildings and their surroundings

Schools are usually housed in fixed buildings within an enclosed environment. Classroom spaces are restricted and reflect the educational ideologies of those controlling them (Goouch, 2005, p19). Children spend the majority of their time in schools indoors – going outdoors into the school grounds, particularly in Key Stages One and Two, is reserved for playtimes, PE and special occasions where connections can be made to children's learning inside the classroom. Going beyond the school grounds is usually a rarely undertaken enterprise which requires permissions, risk assessments and additional adults and is often seen as an end-of-term treat or a stimulus to or consolidation of a topic rather than an integral part of children's learning experiences (Groundwater-Smith, 2004; Bishop and Curtis, 2001; Thornton and Brunton, 2005; Bilton, 2002).

The role of adults

Adults generally lead the learning which takes place in schools, be they government advisers and policy makers, Local Authorities, or headteachers and practitioners. Adults in the classroom are generally perceived as leaders, the source of knowledge, rather than collaborators, guides or 'more knowledgeable other' working alongside children to develop their thinking and their ideas (see Vygotsky, 1978; Wood and Atfield, 1996; Bruce, 2005b).

The curriculum

There is a fixed curriculum which vies with the rhetoric of child-initiated or child-centred learning. On the one hand practitioners are asked to look at the learning needs of individual children yet on the other they are required to ensure that all children meet the same curricular targets – regardless of those very needs. How practitioners balance the needs of the individual against accountability to a prescribed curriculum is at the heart of teaching and learning in the Early Years (see Flinders and Thornton, 1997; Kelly, 1999; Seedfeldt, 1999).

Letting the outside in

Clearly some of the limitations of schools are harder to overcome than others. Nevertheless there are settings where these limits are rigidly upheld and others where the limits are stretched or overcome. Your practice will demonstrate how far you, and the setting where you work, accept or resist the limits imposed upon you. Each chapter in this book offers practical ways in which practitioners can work creatively within these limits – or push at them – to enhance the learning experiences of the children with whom they work. Each author offers a different perspective on how the outside can be brought into the classroom, whether by closing the gap between home and school, or by physically moving beyond the four walls of the classroom.

Ian Shirley and Sue Hammond describe ways in which the school grounds, whatever they offer, can be used to provide enriching experiences in play and creative expression. Terry Whyte, Jonathan Barnes and Gina Donaldson take elements of children's local environments, looking respectively at aspects of geography, music and mathematics in unusual and exciting ways. The concept of forest schools is given a Danish perspective by Jane Williams-Siegfredsen and a British one by Trisha Maynard, suggesting ways in which practitioners can take their practice forward in a principled way, irrespective of the environment within which they work. Richard Bailey and Ian Pickup examine the role of movement in learning, considering the physical needs of children in schools and ways in which movement can be incorporated across the curriculum. Children's absorption in popular culture is addressed by Gill Hope. Taking Design and Technology as a focus, she considers how children's toys can be used to provide worthwhile learning experiences. The role of parents as a significant part of children's lives is explored in my own chapter and I discuss how relationships between parents and practitioners can be developed. Helen Taylor and I go beyond the local community in the next chapter, describing the need for a global perspective in children's education and how this can be linked to the teaching of modern foreign languages. The final chapter by Alan Peacock considers the need to conserve the natural resources which make up outside environment and provides ideas for promoting ecological principles with young children.

Thus many themes and ideas run through and overlap in the book, all of them concerned with enriching children's school experiences by letting the outside in.

1

Exploring the great outdoors

Ian Shirley

The great outdoors

It has always amazed me how differently children behave outside the classroom. Whatever the purpose of going outdoors the children and I always seemed to return in higher spirits. Science investigations, arts activities, sports and data-gathering tasks all became much more relevant the moment we left the sterile world of the classroom. But each of these tasks is usually part of a practitioner initiated activity. How much more relevant and exciting could the learning be for our children if we allowed them to take some of the decisions about spaces to be explored and activities to be undertaken?

Recently, in the centre of a local town I took some time to watch the world go by. Soon I became aware that a large, slightly raised, aluminium circle in the centre of the square was causing a great deal of interest. Children couldn't resist it. They walked along its edge, trying not to fall off; they walked to the centre and jumped hard, testing its springiness and sound qualities; they scraped their shoes along its rough surface. One boy just stood in the centre and admired his new, slightly elevated perspective. Soon I noticed adults, too, were tempted by this object. Some, the responsible ones, walked around it. Some skirted the edge, feeling it beneath their feet, using their senses to get a good feel for the object. Some were openly inquisitive: they strode straight to the middle of the circle with a sure step, thoroughly enjoying the texture of the metal and the spongy bounce of this makeshift playground installation. To me it was a form of community performance art. I enjoyed the way a simple object affected the spirit of these shoppers for a minute – a brief diversion from the hum-drum and predictable activity we call retail therapy.

We should be aware of this phenomenon. Napier and Shankey (in Wyse, 2004) remind us of the importance of the play model of learning developed by Hutt *et al* (1989):

> Without opportunities to explore, the child has a limited knowledge of the materials, their properties and the possibilities of use. Exploration allows children to develop their knowledge, skills and understanding. When these are in place children can progress to more creative or conventional responses. (p150)

It seemed obvious to me that all the shoppers I observed were enjoying the intrinsic pleasure of this exploration process. Human beings are naturally inquisitive and it is up to practitioners to exploit this natural trait. Indeed some pedagogies, such as Reggio Emilia, denounce a given curriculum in favour of a curriculum determined by the child, as Thornton and Brunton (2005) explain:

> In Reggio, there is no predetermined curriculum; children's learning is developed through their involvement in long and short-term projects ...At the centre of the Reggio pedagogy is the child who ...embodies a curiosity and open-mindedness to all that is possible. (p8)

That a simple object, such as the one in the town centre, caused so many people to observe, hypothesise, test and analyse suggests we should be making more use of naturally inquiring minds. It also suggests that novel and unfamiliar situations cause us to question. For this reason, and as already discussed above, practitioners should try to find novel and unfamiliar places for children's investigations. Certainly we need to go outdoors but where might remain unexplored? Every school will differ but locations chosen should be rich in features, safe and appropriate for intended purpose; familiar in outline but unfamiliar in detail. Here are some suggestions of locations that might be worth considering:

- underneath a hedge
- the car park
- under a window ledge
- a porch
- a bench
- a garden
- under a mobile classroom

- a wall of a building
- a tree
- under a stone or other object
- the path to the school
- the pond area
- the bin/skip storage area
- the playground
- the playing fields
- under a bridge
- in a nearby church yard
- the other side of the fence

Getting started

In a recent arts project, students at Canterbury Christ Church University worked together with children in local primary schools. Part of their brief was to investigate the potential of the school grounds for motivating learning across the curriculum. One group had decided to focus on a seemingly dull grassy enclosure. It was a long narrow strip, the size of a regular back garden, protected by a fence on three sides and a low wall which met up with the playground on the other. Beyond one side of the fence lay an attractive and well-maintained garden; the remainder provided a boundary with the outside world. A significant feature of the enclosure was a large tree whose canopy dominated the air-space. Clearly this place was familiar but largely unexplored, rich in feature and, as it was enclosed, safe. No doubt the children noticed this space every day, as it lay very close to their classroom and outdoor play area. The students wanted the children to think about it in a new and highly focused way; they wanted to give the space an identity beyond anything that it had achieved so far. The idea was to develop the garden as a space for wishes – a 'wishing garden' in fact. The medium was to be the arts and the children were encouraged to think about the space through a range of sensitising experiences.

Sensitising experiences

We only make sense of places through action and interaction. Without this kind of experience we cannot know the 'essence' of a place. Such action and interaction involves a process of sensitisation by which places become familiar and understood. We use touch, smell, sight and hearing to reference the space and, consequently, we are able to select spaces for appropriate activities such as taking photographs, playing games, having a picnic, setting a story or holding an outdoor summer concert. In order for the children to design and build the 'wish garden' it was vital that they got to know the space really well first. They needed to know about its shape and form. They needed to experience its atmosphere and to become familiar with the artefacts that made the space special. For this a series of suitable 'sensitising experiences' were undertaken which had the additional benefit of encouraging the children to work collaboratively and, perhaps more importantly, in original and novel ways. Ways that were more related to children's imaginary play than to regular 'content-driven' learning.

Such experiences rely on the children being immersed in an environment through all senses. It is not enough to go on a sound walk and simply talk about what is heard. The children need to be encouraged to select, reject, sort, engage, create, develop and synthesise these sounds. They need to be encouraged to focus on detail. As Shirley Brice-Heath notes:

> [Children's] ... attention to detail runs contrary to established and expected notions of the attention span of very young children. Their shifts in before and after drawings ... attest to children's willingness to look and look again if given the encouragement and ... the chance. (2004, p44)

Perhaps we ought to give ourselves the chance to look again too. The tasks that follow are meant to stimulate interest in and awareness of the environment. While they will certainly work with children, you may equally enjoy doing them yourselves, with colleagues or with your family. One of the greatest joys of teaching is being a lifelong learner and being open to unexpected and unplanned moments of discovery. Rediscover your childlike inquisitiveness and never lose hold of it!

Sounds

Let the children experience the sounds of a place. Unusual spaces can be interesting sites for listening. Encourage them to explore the sound qualities of materials available: beating bins, running a stick along a fence, beating a metal pole with different types of beaters, real and found. Try tapping, flicking and patting with fingers. Explore shouting through pipes and tapping on different lengths of drainpipe. Most importantly, question the children about the noises they make. Get them to use appropriate language to define what they have heard. Talk about timbre – the way different objects sound. Explore what effects the sounds would be good for.

Talk about pitch – how some sounds are higher than others. Get them to notice the connection between size and pitch. Create rhythm phrases. Play echo games and question and answer responses. Get the children to explore loud and quiet. Think about sounds that travel and sounds that are difficult to hear. Create maps of a sound walk through the space or plot sounds on a spatialisation plan like the one given below.

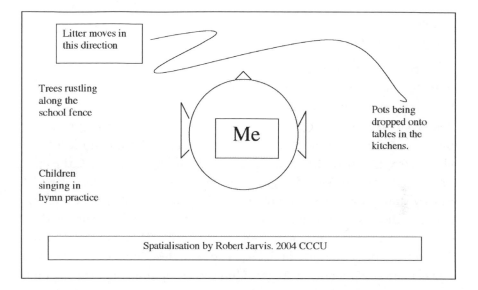

Spatialisation by Robert Jarvis. 2004 CCCU

Many artists use such sounds to create soundscapes that suggest the nature of a place or an idea. The sounds can be collected on a simple tape recorder or, more interestingly, on a digital recording device. They can be analysed and described in terms of their main features and children may enjoy guessing what these sounds are. The children could be invited to produce a graphic score, showing the sounds as they appear, like a piece of music. Older children may go on to manipulating these sounds with simple computer programmes such as Windows 'sound recorder'. They can loop the sounds, play them in different directions and add echo effects before they are added to acoustic instruments as part of a musical composition.

The ultimate aim of this is to make children sound-aware so they enhance their familiarity with spaces they encounter every day. They can then make decisions about suitable spaces based on the sound environment they will be working in.

Sights

Encourage the children to notice what they see in these spaces. Allow them to work in twos, taking each other to interesting places, each child positioning the other carefully to notice something interesting exactly as they want it to be seen. One child could lead the other, eyes closed, and then squeeze their hand for as long as their eyes are to be open. They should be encouraged to describe accurately what they have seen. They should use words about colour, size, shape and texture to achieve real and cognisant sensitisation to the place.

Cameras are a useful and familiar device for getting to know a place. Set a limit to the number or types of photographs that can be taken. For example, ask children to take ten photographs that feature a shape or a colour. Or take ten photographs that reflect the atmosphere of a place. The children should work in groups and there should be much discussion about what photographs are to be taken. Digital imaging allows the children to accept and reject images more freely. You might want to restrict this by stating that they can only reject two pictures. All others must be carefully discussed and prepared before the shots are taken. The children could provide a presentation of their photographs. They can describe the features of a place they like or dislike. They can describe their reactions to a place and discuss how feelings within the group differed. Once again it is important to focus on the detail and help the children find words that express their thoughts and intentions. Imagine the discussion that could erupt over an upturned bin, or a building half demolished or half built.

Get the children to identify places where two interesting materials meet, such as where a piece of bark has been stripped away on a tree. Contrasting materials, juxtaposed, provide an interesting resource for close observational drawing. Focus on colour, texture and contrast and encourage the children to enjoy the interesting effects created by both natural and man-made objects. In focusing on such detail you will help the children to become observant and fastidious in their approach to all aspects of their work.

Ask them to collect items from around the space which are of special significance and provide something of the essence of the space. These could be used in a collage or as visual aids in a display of poetry. Use the objects as a basis for literacy. Ask the children to describe them in detail, on paper or to a friend. Play a game of 'guess who I am' or write riddles, where the person describing has to try to keep the identity of the object hidden, but nevertheless has to tell the truth. This will help them focus on the smallest details of the object.

The ultimate aim of all this is to make children visually aware. They will become used to looking for the detail and observant enough to suggest suitable spaces for a variety of activities in the future.

Concepts

We learn by touching, smelling, hearing, seeing and responding emotionally and spiritually to stimuli. We can reinforce the experience by talking, reading, and writing, but the starting points have to be direct, personal experiences. (from *The Coombes School Handbook* in Jeffrey and Woods, 2003, p28)

Coombes School in Berkshire places equal value on learning outdoors and in, as this extract from its Handbook illustrates. Emphasis is on helping children understand what has been learnt. Equally, we should be looking for opportunities for children to notice their responses to spaces and activities throughout their tasks. So we need to encourage children to think about how they are affected by the activities and the spaces they are working in; that is, to consider the emotional charge of a space. Such thoughts encourage aesthetic awareness, and this not only helps children become cultured and thoughtful but can have a significant role in their spiritual development (see Radford, 2004, p87 for further discussion).

Ask the children to consider the place in a novel way. Perhaps they could collect photographs featuring a chosen number, such as study of 'Three' or maybe they could investigate shades of colour, such as a study in 'Yellow'. These could then be used as an introduction to the work of artists such as Paul Klee, who became obsessed with colour.

Ask the children to consider their emotional response to different places. Ask them to find comfortable places, sad places, scary places, peaceful places. Allow them to draw these places, perhaps getting them to think about how colour can help to create an atmosphere. Then get them to photograph the places using a variety of techniques, such as colour photography, black and white photography and close-up shots. Use the pictures for a class discussion about their feelings and to compare their findings.

Move a stone in a damp area and ask the children to watch the activity of minibeasts closely. They should sit and listen quietly, noting the different forms of movement of the creatures, their appearance and activities. Ask them to make suggestions about life under the stone. What are the characteristics of the creatures? Who's the boss? Who are the naughty ones? Get them to sketch one creature. Get them to take close-up photographs with zoom-lens cameras. The very act of getting down and dirty in the mud and clay provides sensory experiences children need. The conversations and shared experiences help to develop a community of researchers who are keen to find out about the world and who build on each others' knowledge and opinions.

Rich tasks

Once internalised, these observations can become synthesised in a rich task. An associate and creative pedagogue, Peter Dixon, suggested many delightful activities to help children learn through play and exploration. One memorable activity was to provide each child with a small chunk of clay so that they could go into the school grounds to find (create) a beautiful bird or fearsome monster. The children would collect materials and stick them into the clay. They had to provide accurate details for their creation, such as its common and scientific names, feeding habits, life cycle and other notable features.

I once did this activity with student teachers. They produced some beautiful and exotic birds which were celebrated in a variety of performances such as a Buddhist-style homage on the university lawn, and a Bill Oddie style nature programme in the science department gardens. Similar opportunities could be provided for young children by inviting them to create a dance for the creatures with musical accompaniment. They should be reminded of how the minibeasts moved so they can decide the kinds of movements to use in their dance. If this is to be a dance about birds they need to spend time watching birds, in the air and on the ground. It should be possible to create a bird hide in the school grounds, perhaps behind a set of steps or near a tree.

Older children could create nature programmes, lasting no longer than two minutes, using video cameras and the movie facility on digital cameras and mobile phones. Again, they should be encouraged to focus on the detail and to plan the action carefully in advance, but only after they have had chance to explore and play first. They could use a story board to present their developing ideas and groups of children could be encouraged to compose incidental music.

Collect the children's emotional responses to places by producing a huge, wall-sized display in the form of a map, where individual groups' feelings are plotted. These can be illustrated by their drawings and photographs and by the objects collected from the spaces. The very process of making such a display is a rich learning opportunity. Capture the conversations, the small acts of collaboration and the creative moments and reinforce these by rewarding the children as they are observed.

Such rich tasks allow children to make decisions about their own learning. You should allow them to get on with the tasks uninterrupted, only stepping in to keep the activity going and to show you value what they are doing. Sometimes you may need to contribute more to help a group move on. The temptation is to take over by giving specific directions. Usually it is more useful to ask questions that provoke the children to think, or even encouraging them to backtrack so that threads can be picked up and redirected. Either way, the benefits of such work is that the children have a strong sense of ownership

Student teachers are often anxious about embarking on activities of this kind and express fear of coping with children's behaviour outside the classroom. However, many are surprised by how engaged the children are outdoors. Experience suggests that if the activities are fun, engaging and worthwhile, behaviour will not be an issue. Children are naturally inquisitive. They learn through observing, testing and accommodating behaviour. Margaret Donaldson (1978, p113) sums up these fundamental urges as 'to be effective, competent and independent, to understand the world and to act with skill'. If we are to truly allow our children to learn and to become independent beings we must provide opportunities for them to exercise control and to make decisions in groups and on their own. As Donaldson observes:

> It is arguable that in some ways we do not encourage competence – that we keep our children too dependent for too long, denying them the opportunity to exercise their very considerable capacity for initiative and responsible action. (*ibid*)

Allow the children to talk in groups and pairs. Show them you value their thoughts and discussions. Working in unusual spaces, away from classrooms, allows children to converse and explore without fear of disturbing other classes. The children will need to negotiate tasks and processes in order to move ahead. They will have to plan together and discuss their findings. They will have to use appropriate language to communicate nuance and to find ways of sharing their findings with the rest of the group. They may need to find ways of expressing the characteristics of a place to the whole class.

Find a reason to congratulate each child and make a point of stressing why their actions and achievements are good. Use domain-specific language to articulate the actual nature of their success and be prepared to step in and show good practice at any point during the activity. Commending children in this way not only provides them with a clear understanding of what good work looks like but also gives them a reason go on. Simply believing you are good at something has a significant effect on actually becoming good at something.

Conclusion

The outside world offers a context for many of the activities children do and we shouldn't overlook the unfamiliar aspects of familiar places. Of course, we can view such places scientifically: we can draw them, measure them, record them, describe them, discuss them and analyse them. But we can also use the magic that is inherent in such places. We can play in them, perform in them, change them, transform them, redesign them, recreate them, speculate about them and represent them. We can try to remember how we used all kinds of places as settings for our own play as children. Our skill as practitioners allows us to step in to make appropriate interjections that will help move children on in their learning. We must try to provide a scaffold to support their learning through listening and observing but we must not hijack their ideas.

We practitioners should seek the potential of our school grounds and local environment to facilitate learning. We should provide opportunities for the children to take decisions about their learning and to take ownership of their curriculum. The school and all it represents is an important part of childhood. Even the more unusual locations need to be explored, demystified and valued if we are to encourage children to become creative and responsive to the ever changing world. We need opportunities to throw off the shackles of our over-prescriptive curriculum in order to do this. The answer may be to extend an approach to education more in keeping with the Foundation Stage as is becoming policy in Wales. For it is at this stage that we see teaching and learning as more in tune with one another. If only governments would defer to practitioners.

Sadly, as Wragg remarked (2004, p98), this couldn't happen in England because 'trust in professionals is simply missing'. So how can we maintain children's 'enthusiasm ... imagination, playfulness, resourcefulness and genuine creativity' (Wyse, 2004, p128) throughout all stages of the primary phase? True engagement for adults and children alike is derived from an inner drive. I do not propose that simply moving children's learning outdoors will magically enhance learning. My contention is that exploring, playing in and re-inventing familiar and unfamiliar places that are easily accessible, near and free will foster genuine creativity, inquisitiveness and the construction of learning.

2

Taking the inside out

Sue Hammond

Introduction

Where do you go to relax? A straw poll of parents and teachers revealed that although shopping, restaurants, cinemas and theatres do feature, their favourite pastimes included being by the sea, strolling through woods or forests, or amidst hills and mountains. Some spoke eloquently of their love of undulating landscapes and green pastures, of the sense of openness and freedom, peace and tranquillity of hill walking. Others were almost lyrical in their praise of the soothing sounds and sights of gleaming, rippling waters, rolling waves and golden sands, or of crunching through leaves as sunlight cascaded through branches.

Amongst your treasured memories of childhood adventures you may recall building dens, bridges or dams with friends, or conquering the steepest hill in order to slide down it. For many of us these were joyous moments during which we developed our social relationships and learnt about our environment, but they may also reflect an innate human affinity to nature. Harvard biochemist Wilson (1984) referred to 'Biophilia' as 'the connections that human beings subconsciously seek with the rest of life' (Kellert and Wilson, 1984). Psychological research has shown that we associate the colour green with a natural world of calmness, freshness and healing and this knowledge is used in the planning of public places such as hospitals and supermarkets.

Nevertheless, there is ambivalence about the relationship between humans and the environment: it brings us riches and pleasures but can destroy us; we seek to respect it but also to control it. It seems, too, that as societies develop we create barriers between ourselves and the natural world – we place pieces of leather around our feet, we build concrete shelters to protect us from the elements – and yet we also find great solace in removing our shoes to walk barefoot across the sand. What is indisputable is that climate change and threats to biodiversity have made it vital that children be aware of the effects of human action on the environment, and educated to enjoy, value and preserve the earth's resources.

In his chapter in this book, Terry Whyte talks about our favourite places of childhood and the development of understanding of the geography of the environment. My intention is to invoke contexts, scenes and events from childhood alongside the emotions and sensual experiences that are associated with them. By doing this, we can begin to appreciate how important such opportunities are for our own children and consider how we can maximise the learning potential and a sense of caring. A further aim is to promote a metaphorical removal of the walls between the outside and indoor spaces and to challenge the view that the enclosed classroom is the place where the important learning occurs. To maximise the potential of the space available the outside classroom will require planning but this should be considered within the wider social and cultural context and through parents and practitioners working together.

Many of the fields and hills that were the natural playgrounds of previous generations have disappeared and the lack of space has been compounded by parental concerns about safety, so children have little opportunity to play freely outdoors. Instead they spend most of their time indoors or in controlled, adult constructed environments. Yet when we examine children's spontaneous responses to the outdoor environment, it is clear that it offers diverse and abundant learning contexts. A young child will delight in the movement of a bird or an insect for an astonishing amount of time; or experiment with the properties of water, soil or twigs; or explore the nooks and crannies amongst rocks and trees. Through these experiences they are developing their knowledge not only of the world around them but of the patterns of life, the potential of different materials, awareness of shape, texture and space and how to concentrate, create and manipulate.

A sensitive adult will listen when children are playing out these scenes and tailor their responses to extend individual learning according to each child's interest at the time. These are likely to be influenced by the child's developmental stage but also by their cultural understandings: 'Culture is both the context *within* which the child develops and the context *into* which the child develops' (Walsh, 2005, p15). It is widely accepted that learning is constructed within a social and cultural framework (Anning *et al*, 2004) and both the curriculum and teaching should be founded on that knowledge. Children use language and make meaning in many different ways and it cannot be denied that working collaboratively with children, in an equal partnership, is a difficult skill for practitioners. Indeed, Bruce (2005a) argues that, 'Intuition is based on an edifice of knowledge,' (p63) and 'only a few skilled practitioners seem to join free-flow play and develop it without destroying it' (p89). But intuition is worth mastering and can be made considerably easier if time is given to nurturing mean-ingful relationships with children and parents and familiarisation with the community. Interactions then become more rewarding and planning future contexts simpler.

The UK government has recognised the contribution made by the outdoor environment to children's learning and physical, emotional and social welfare and has consequently allocated funding for initiatives such as Forest Schools (see later chapters) and Woodland areas and for developing the outdoor space as a key area in the Foundation Stage. This last is prov-ing a huge challenge for many primary schools and is to be the main con-text discussed in this chapter.

Where do I begin?

What are the starting points for planning an outdoor space? Do you look at what is available and plan from there? Do you start with the Early Learn-ing Goals (DfEE/QCA, 2000) and consider how these will best be achieved? Do you look at the budget and rapidly conclude that it is inadequate?

It is fair to say that outdoor spaces have only recently become a wide-spread educational priority. Before, many school fields and open areas had been built upon or sold off, so just finding suitable ground can be dif-ficult. Once found, the practicalities of access between the inside and out-side classroom, cost, health and safety, supervision and the demands of the curriculum can seem overwhelming. In an educational system in which we have become increasingly accountable, each of these factors has to be addressed, but it is important that they are a secondary considera-tion rather than the driver of the planning process. Planning is exciting and excitement for developing an outside classroom comes from the chance to imaginatively combine knowledge of children's learning and well-being with the creation of a space that incorporates opportunities and materials to enrich them. Malone and Tranter (2003) consider the design of the outdoor space as

> ...the 'stage' where children act out, spontaneously and freely, the events that touch their lives. It is the space where they connect with the social, cultural and ecological domains of childhood. (p289)

Therefore, at the heart of the planning process are children and how they learn and what we would like them to learn; in particular, their learning dispositions and their respect for the world about them, rather than pre-determined outcomes. If children are truly to be at the core of this process their voices need to be heard and we should be asking children about the environments in which they like to learn. Lancaster (2006) describes this as a 'Rights-based approach', referring to the United Nations Convention (UNICEF, 1989) and the *Every Child Matters* (DfES, 2004) agenda that encapsulate the right of children to express opinions, to be listened to and to play. Asking the opinions of young children can be time-consuming and conversations are not always straightforward, but we can also learn much about their preferences from watching and listening to them during their play.

The children interviewed and observed for the purposes of this chapter favoured:

- Areas to play with fundamental elements such as sand and water
- Space to ride or use wheeled vehicles
- The chance to make camps or 'play hiding'
- Interesting things to look at such as animals, plants and insects
- Somewhere to run and move about 'and play football with my friends'

Their opinions provide the basis for the following suggestions in what is envisioned as a series of outside rooms for different activities, interconnected by pathways and planting to create flow and atmosphere.

An environment for learning

From a child's viewpoint natural elements such as sand, water, plants and minibeasts are essential and these appear to be popular regardless of ethnicity, culture or social experience. Furthermore, although some young children may develop a dislike for getting dirty or a fear of spiders or heights, most children love to experiment with mud, to observe a minibeast scavenging in a rotting log and to climb and take risks. These are part of the wonder and work of childhood, involving active learning through real and rich experiences. Some natural materials are now available in indoor and outdoor classrooms and it has been reassuring to see sand and water becoming accepted parts of the learning curriculum in Early Years' settings, instead of a reward for completing a written task. So I'm advocating the inclusion of a few of the materials that have received little attention and to evaluate them from the perspective of their appeal to children and the contribution to their development and understanding.

Mud

Earth in its various forms is rich in potential for learning. Mud, clay, dry soil and compost are cheap, versatile and each has a different part to play in the outside space. It has to be mud, because of its connotations of oozing and stickiness, its wonderful texture and potential for moulding or trickling between fingers and squelching between toes. The therapeutic and cleansing powers of mud have a long history that has achieved scientific authentication and, although it cannot be claimed that all mud has such effects, there is something delightfully soothing and calming about it. So it can be claimed that it contributes to children's well-being.

The things a child does with the mud will invariably be affected by their cultural and social experience as well as the affordances of the material. The following two examples offer anecdotal evidence to support this. The first involved a group of four four and five year olds in a Kent primary school. They put the mud they found in the corner of the school playing field to good use in playtime. They made cakes, each with a cherry on the top and they created a race track for the toy cars they brought from home tucked in their pockets. In the second scenario, three girls in South India were delighted to find a damp patch of mud in their parched, dusty play ground. They used it to form a three-sided structure to represent a Hindu shrine that they carefully decorated with flowers, twigs and leaves.

Whatever the differences in their creations, these children were all totally absorbed in their tasks and in expanding their understanding of the properties of soil. It is easy to dismiss such events and view children's play at a superficial level but deeper analysis often yields insights into their burgeoning scientific, mathematic and geographic knowledge, their narratives and the processes of socialisation and creativity. When four year old Gavin experimented with his car in the mud, his concentration and commentary centred on the tracks it formed, how they differed in width and pattern to those of his friends' vehicles, changed in appearance where the surface was drier, and had to be pushed harder where the mud was spongier. Playing in parallel beside him, Oliver related a story that reflected and interwove some of Gavin's observations so that the cars raced each other, then became stuck and finally reached the finish line 'with mud all over the wheels'.

The comments of the girls in India, spoken in Tamil, were less accessible but it was clear that they were using their shrine as a backdrop for a role play in which one girl was the Swami and the others were worshippers bearing offerings. They made creative use of the wild flowers and natural materials in their environment to equip their shrine with a Puja tray, Arti lamp, candles, bells and statues.

Children in such scenarios are making connections with previously acquired, socially embedded knowledge and forming a foundation for future experiences and learning. They are collaboratively reconstructing and reinventing, creating narratives and connecting with their cultural history. With support, they will be able to extend their awareness to know, for instance, that the clay that stubbornly adheres to the wheels of the car or is shaped into a shrine can be used for all sorts of purposes and has since prehistoric times provided shelter, cooking and storage pots, dishes for eating and a plethora of artistic, spiritual and decorative items. The role of the practitioner may be to co-construct the learning by posing puzzles or providing additional materials and sharing in the play, and later introducing the next area of focus: that of growing, with seeds and bulbs.

Vegetation
Intrinsically associated with soil are plants and vegetation and they, too, are essential to an aesthetically pleasing, environmentally friendly, educational place. Plants are important in helping parents and practitioners to educate children about respecting and caring for the environment. At one level, we are aware that plants enhance the landscape with their beauty, nourish with their fruits, leaves and seeds and can heal or relax us with their perfumes, colours and medicinal qualities. However, as an enduring investment, we need to nurture a deeper level of respect for the ecosystem and for sustainable use of the earth's resources.

How many of us have memories of blissful summer days in childhood when we removed the silken, fading petals from roses and blended them with water to manufacture a sweet, transient perfume? Or delicately pierced the stems of daisies to link them together to form chains from which to make crowns, necklaces and decorative garlands? Although such activities may not lead to careers in perfumery or floristry, they can contribute to such interpersonal skills as cooperation and negotiation; to fine muscle control; to knowledge of irreversible changes and decomposition, and an array of sensory perceptions. The challenge for adults involved with children is to find ways of capitalising on the events and enriching the learning without detracting from the enjoyment or wonder. Furthermore, when we evoke such memories they are invariably associated with scents, tactile sensations and emotional stimuli that can lead to deep-seated learning.

Sensory gardens have received much attention recently and many schools have developed areas that incorporate trees, flowers and herbs that offer physical and environmental benefits. Growing plants from seeds, cuttings or bulbs helps children to learn about them and about caring for them. Growing foods such as carrots, parsley, or lettuces invite talk about their nutritional value, shape, size, texture, root systems etc. The children enjoy making description labels and charting the plants' growth. Wild flowers and leaves attract butterflies and other wildlife into the area and so enhance the environment as well as contributing to children's understanding and discussion.

The space available for these areas may be small so decisions have to be made to rotate flowers and crops or use the soil in different ways, but setting aside a small area of land for growing offers flexibility and diversity. Existing trees, plants and shrubs provide some of the places requested by children for climbing over, under and through and for dens and hiding. At a nursery in Sweden, for example, children and staff were growing willow whips and training them to form an arched tunnel to crawl through and hide under. They regularly checked the tree's progress and patiently tended it; they delighted in carefully moving through it without touching and damaging the growth. Willow is robust and some varieties grow vigorously so it can be perfect for creating arbours and playhouses. Honeysuckle or yew can be used to create mazes. Tall flowers such as poppies, sunflowers, foxgloves and campion create magical areas for weaving and running in or curling up quietly. Malaguzzi, founder of the Reggio Emilia preschools, advocated spaces for children where the grass is taller than they are and most of us can recall such places we enjoyed for solitude and quiet reflection.

Boxes

Although trees, shrubs and grasses provide perfect canopies, a blanket placed across a clothes drier or a large cardboard box can be equally effective. Boxes of different shapes and sizes are notoriously popular playthings for young children and a versatile addition to the outdoor space. Reusing packaging materials is better for the environment than adding them to landfill. In one primary school boxes and tubes have had numerous lives as Santa's sleigh, garages, boats, spaceships and much else. My three-year-old son had months of pleasure from a robust cardboard box left over from moving house. After I had cut a door and window, he painted it with the remains from tins of emulsion paint and grew pots of herbs around the base. We adapted large sheets of plastic to protect it from the rain and he, his friends and teddies enjoyed many adventures in and around it. Here, part of the parental role was to provide skills that my child had not yet acquired to help him achieve his intentions. He drew on his cultural knowledge of homes and gardens to decide on what he wanted and together we recycled various materials and pooled ideas to create a space for him that was personal, safe and fairly waterproof.

Protecting boxes from the elements can be managed by using heavy gauge plastic, which is widely available, for groundsheets, gazebos and other garden furniture. Gazebos provide inexpensive sun protection for children too, although shrubs, trees or a more permanent pergola or awning might be preferable.

Getting out there

During wet or cold weather, appropriate clothing and footwear should be all children need to explore outside and have fun. Tucked away in your memory bank somewhere must be an agreeable picture of splashing in puddles or of the fascination when you saw your breath form a smoky vapour on frosty mornings. Such experiences are perfect for developing children's scientific knowledge, for co-constructing a story and for physical exploration. Children are programmed from birth to be on the move and exploring, and it seems counterproductive to insist that they sit for long periods in order to be educated. As child psychologists Gopnik, Meltzof and Kuhl (1999) say:

> The rapid and profound changes in children's understanding of the world seem related to the ways they explore and experiment. Children actively do things to promote their understanding of disappearances, causes and categories. (p86)

It is through their interactions with the environment that children learn about it and the objects within it and develop their own physical capabilities. One of the dilemmas facing Early Years' practitioners is how to offer children activities that involve climbing, balancing, swinging and sliding and carry elements of risk in a culture where there are constant attempts to eliminate accidents. It seems that humans are predisposed towards risk-taking and Factor (2004) and Stephenson (2003) both found evidence that children would create their own challenges and subvert the use of 'safe' playground equipment. This is borne out by my own video tape of primary school children using a solid wooden, safety-marked, climbing frame and slide: after they had obeyed the rule of removing their shoes and socks, they used the structure to act out a gun chase, dogs fighting, create a hideout and undertake various precarious manoeuvres. Factor (2004) suggests that children have the 'capacity to utilise materials at hand and the available space (including areas not intended for play) for their own inventive and imaginative purposes' (p4), and adults cannot legislate against this. Expensive equipment does not guarantee children's safety – nor the direction of their learning.

It is environmentally and practically sensible to use the natural landscape and consider its potential for physical play. In some European settings this includes rocks and hills for climbing, scrambling, hiding and sliding. Logs, bark, pebbles or tree stumps are all versatile materials that can be moved around to form stepping stones, tracks and balancing points. Where the area is an uninviting concrete wasteland it may be desirable to create timber frames in which to rotate materials and to use tubs and pots to soften the lines until a permanent solution is agreed and financed.

Although this chapter is mostly about sustainable and natural materials and environments, this does not mean I subscribe to the view that man-made items are worthless. Bicycles and buggies, pulleys and cogs, bricks and construction kits, ropes and balls, dolls and dressing-up clothes, are just a few of the manufactured items that can enrich children's imaginative, inventive and exploratory play. But children will adapt what there is and use their playfulness to symbolise and create meaning.

Conclusion

Whatever the external environment, the consensus emerging from research by Bishop and Curtis (2003), David *et al* (2005), Factor (2004) and Titman (1994) is that the greatest contribution to young children's healthy development and learning comes from 'loving, responsive, sensitive key people' (David *et al*, 2005, p54) who provide the physical and emotional space for them to think and feel, to plan and work at something, to be with others or alone, to metaphorically or literally ask questions. Parents and practitioners working together can provide an outdoor classroom that is rich and vibrant, planned in harmony with its natural contours and contents, where children will dynamically and joyfully engage in their learning.

3

Personal geographies – children and their local environment

Terry Whyte

Introduction

Have you ever looked into your past and remembered a favourite place where you used to play or where you particularly liked to go? Was it a field or woodland, or a play park or a favourite room in a house, like Gran's bedroom or Dad's shed, a street, a back garden, a yard? Most of us have such favourite places tucked away at the backs of our minds, places we used to explore, feel safe, comfortable and happy in, playing with friends and relatives or alone. Children have their own favourite places, their personal geographies, which they talk about with affection.

Interaction with the immediate environment is important for children's emotional well-being and educational development. Hart's (1979) work on personal geographies concluded that children valued features that met their physical and emotional needs. These were places where they often met other children or familiar adults, could explore and play in, places where pathways and alleyways were formed and intertwined with make believe play and games. Do adults' memories of favourite childhood places also have strong associations with playing? Children's favourite places can have meaning that may seem strange to an adult; often children prefer a well worn corner of a field with a fallen tree to carefully designed and expensive playgrounds.

When exploring geographical concepts with children and describing physical and human landscapes, practitioners have a responsibility to take account of the personal element – the children's responses to and understanding of their environment should work to enhance their knowledge of that environment. By engaging with their personal geographies, we can develop children's knowledge and understanding of their world and the wider world.

Concerns

Whilst children usually have a sound knowledge of their own home environment, they are not necessarily given the opportunity to explore or create a personal geography connected with their outside environment. At a time when there are perceived dangers for children plus the real dangers inherent in increased road traffic, schools need to help promote knowledge of the environment lest these 'dangers' prevent children from physically interacting with it.

In 1993, Hillman reported that the number of unaccompanied activities undertaken by junior age school children at weekends had halved between 1971 and 1990. Arguably this figure continues to fall as local streets and the areas of playgrounds with, for example, fallen trees that have invested meanings are often perceived as areas of risk. The world outside could consequently become even more removed from children's direct experience especially when within the safe home environment, images of the 'outside' from around the world are seen through images on television, computers and DVDs. In a way, the personal geographies of today's young children may be worldwide but unconnected with what is on their doorstep. Owens (2004) argues that many young children seem can name television characters, McDonald's menus lists and so on without effort but struggle to name three birds or flowers. Bowles (1998) warns that if learning experiences from being outdoors are not repeated and developed in school and beyond then much of what is learned may be forgotten.

Travelling by car to nearby places and from home to school inhibits children's knowledge of connections and links. Sibley (1995) suggests that children know their locality from the car in the company of adults rather than from being alone or in the company of other children. 'The car then functions as a protective capsule from which the child observes the world but does not experience it directly' (p136). Furthermore, children's observation of the world from a car window is slight, especially when the journey is along a regular route. The differences between walking a route and being driven are manifold: the physical experience children gain in walking, the interactions with objects and other people, the sensory experiences, all make walking an experience that contributes to their personal geographies and can be incorporated into their learning in the classroom.

Ross (2004) highlighted the positive effects on children when they participate in their local communities. His research showed the strong sense of belonging these children had. They could name their favourite places or friends in the local area and 'children were more able to develop a sense of responsibility'. This is echoed by the Living Streets campaign (2005), which called for children to be allowed to explore the opportunities of the area in which they live. It points out that children who are allowed to play in the streets by themselves develop strong social relationships with other children and adults and can entertain themselves for much longer than children accompanied by adults. Parents, though, tend to keep their children indoors to protect them against much publicised incidents and road traffic. Roads, streets and lanes are perceived as unsafe places to play.

While some children are restricted, there are others who come to school with a well developed knowledge of their local environment, because they are allowed to roam freely around where they live with little adult supervision. In such circumstances children have a sense of belonging to their neighbourhood even if they do not always treat it responsibly.

It is important for Early Years' practitioners and geography teachers to enable children to share experiences of the outdoor environment. Meaningful explorations can thus be jointly developed with teachers and peers in order to build a sense of place.

The Foundation Stage and beyond

Good provision for learning in the Foundation Stage will also involve a range of outdoor and indoor learning opportunities, a variety of resources and a clear underpinning ethic. Young children need to be exposed to a range of experiences that engage curiosity, invite physical and sensory exploration and provide opportunities for them to evaluate and change their environment. (Martin and Owens, 2004, p73)

Spencer (2004) argues that the subject of geography and teaching in the Early Years can feature strongly in partnerships with parents and peers and personal exploration of the neighbourhood. He links the importance of geography teaching in enhancing personal well-being to issues of community and citizenship, thus reflecting the requirement of the main areas of the Foundation Stage curriculum to make children aware of their place in the world and help them make sense of the world.

The Geographical Association's (GA) position statement of 2003 urges that children be enabled to make sense of their place in the world, and recommends that:

- children are inspired to think about their values, their rights and responsibilities to other people and the environment and given opportunities to participate
- children's knowledge, understandings and feelings about people and places are drawn upon by practitioners
- children are supported and encouraged to construct their own meanings about people and places
- children are encouraged to identify other peoples and places in positive ways
- practitioners recognise that children's sense of identity is rooted in the places they live and play
- children's home areas, families and communities are valued
- children actively experience a variety of high quality stimulating environments

Geography takes its place within the area of learning of Knowledge and Understanding of the World in the Foundation Stage curriculum (DfEE/QCA, 2000) – a good description of the subject of geography at all levels. Within a holistic Early Years' curriculum geographical activities naturally provide opportunities for learning across all areas, through the physical play and exploration of the shape and space around them, through developing attitudes towards and creative responses to the environment.

Enquiry

Children need to have first hand experiences of outdoors and teachers need to involve children in observing, asking questions and communicating with others. Practitioners can engage with attitudes children have towards their environment, whether positive or negative, and perhaps challenge some preconceived ideas they may have of the world around them.

Certain questions can help with the process of geographical enquiry for example: Where is this place? What is this place like? What is it like to be here? But essentially the exploration of children's worlds can be more effectively discovered through observing and talking about what they see, feel and experience outdoors; this helps make links with their personal geographies and in forming higher order questions and lines of enquiry in later years. Even for very young children, an enquiry approach can assist children in managing their own learning, with support from others.

The main aims when exploring the outdoor environment in the Early Years would be to observe, find out and identify features in the place they live and the natural world and to find out about their local environment and talk about the features they like and dislike.

Houses and homes

Houses and homes are very personal spaces for young children and adults alike. It is the place where many things happen, where relationships for young children are forged, where understanding of systems, routines and patterns are interpreted and operated but it is above all where shelter is provided and children are clothed, fed and hopefully feel secure and loved. The home forms a large part of a child's personal geography and should be used to good effect by practitioners in the Early Years' environment. Practitioners spend much time in helping children to feel safe and secure in the classroom environment without necessarily accepting what is in the minds of the children that makes them feel the same way in their home environment. Asking questions about home and what it means to children brings the outside into the classroom, and is contextually and emotionally engaging.

Questions to ask might be:

- What is your home like?
- Who lives there?
- Can you describe your home?
- Can you describe some of the rooms?
- What is your favourite part of the house?
- Have you a garden? What is it like?

Looking at other children's homes in the vicinity encourages children to think about other people and the way they live. Questions might be:

- What are the houses made of?
- What do the people who live there do?
- What are the front doors like?
- What are the gardens like?
- Have the people got any pets?
- How is the house painted and decorated?

- Does the house have television/satellite?
- Is this house like yours?
- Do you like this house?

When they look at houses and homes in the street children could:

- make drawings
- take photographs
- take video
- make tape recordings
- interview people
- count features

Back in the classroom they might:

- talk about the people who might live in the houses
- talk about the real people who live in the houses
- talk with the real people who live in the houses
- pretend to be the people in the houses
- examine the photographs and video taken
- make the houses and streets out of building blocks or other materials
- create or draw the gardens
- attempt to draw simple maps of their own home and other houses
- make elementary maps large and small to locate the houses
- explore the stories and rhymes of people who live in the different houses
- begin to explore the different houses seen around the world
- talk about their houses and homes and look at similarities and differences

The streets

In the streets, children encounter the buildings, spaces and places that make up the built environment around them. Children are familiar with their own homes but less so with other buildings and other people's homes in the neighbouring streets. How much do they notice about the landmarks and spaces in their local area? Even if children do walk rather than drive through the streets, do they really observe what is around them or does familiarity mean that they don't? By looking at roads, streets and lanes, children can build knowledge and understanding of the local environment that links with the school and its location in their world. The questions to ask might be:

- What are the buildings in the streets?
- What are they used for?
- What are the different uses of the buildings: homes, shops, surgeries etc?
- What jobs do the people who work in the buildings do?
- Who lives or works in them?
- How old or new are the buildings?
- Are they attractive?
- What might be around the back of the buildings?
- What do the children like or dislike about the buildings they see?
- What are the surfaces on the buildings like – rough, smooth, patterned...?
- What is the roof like?
- What can be seen on the ground? Gratings, bins, kerbs etc
- What notices do the children recognise?
- What vehicles can be seen?
- Is the street busy or quiet?
- Is it tidy or untidy?
- Are there spaces in the streets? What are they used for?
- What is the landscape of the street like? Is it on a hill or is it flat?
- What natural features can be seen in the street – trees, bushes, pond?
- Are the streets surrounded by other streets or by fields, hedges, cliffs, rivers?

The activities for work in the streets and back in the classroom are similar to those for homes. Children might:

- talk about the people they have seen in the street
- talk about the different buildings
- draw pictures of different buildings
- make a tally chart of different buildings
- describe what it is like to walk down the street, using simple geographical language

- draw some notices and signs
- consider the jobs the people in the streets do
- link these jobs with jobs that may be found in streets around the world
- read stories or look at videos about streets
- sing songs about streets
- make a large picture of 'Our Street'

People and jobs

The places around where children live are connected with people and it is important for practitioners and children to realise this. By considering local people and their place in the community, children can begin building connections to their locality and an understanding about how the community itself works. The link with home and school and the jobs local people have can be strengthened by encouraging children to look around them. It will help children understand that the community is made up of people from all walks of life, all races, religions and ages.

Specific jobs and services could be investigated with emphasis on working with the people who carry these out. For instance visits could be made to:

- individual shops
- supermarkets
- doctors' and dentists' surgeries
- museums
- fire and police stations
- libraries
- farms

Such visits afford a wealth of information which can be gathered in various ways and brought back into the classroom. The experience of being with adults who help to put out fires, and of climbing onto a fire engine is exciting. And handling the equipment people in supermarkets use for checking stock, or lying in a dental chair is contextual and concrete and should enable a lot of talk, animation and fun back in class. They might follow up with:

- role play about the different jobs people do
- developing specific role play areas based on the concrete experiences

- relate the jobs they saw to people they know from home and family
- drawing and painting
- stories and rhymes connected with jobs and occupations

Visits by people to the school are also helpful. People from all walks of life can come and talk and share something of their lives with the children. This could concern specific occupations or involve people with certain skills eg singers, actors, puppeteers, or simply people of various ages talking about their lives. Some might even be working in a different part of the school, like a volunteer helper or caretaker.

The environment

By looking at the outside environment children will find out about their locality. When they talk about the features they like and dislike children will probably observe and describe features that can evoke greater environmental appreciation. By being outside they might notice, perhaps for the first time, how untidy the streets are, how noisy and dangerous. Or they might appreciate the beauty of the environment and notice new, exciting things. Either way, children can begin relating to what is around them and form their own opinions about their experience. Thus even at an early age, they become interested young citizens whose personal geographies are developing beyond what they initially brought to school from home. Specific activities will encourage the process, such as:

- looking at pollution around the school or outside (see Chapter 12)
- looking at wildlife habitats
- counting the various forms of wildlife they see
- walking along themed trails in urban and rural areas
- helping make a play area
- getting involved in locating bird boxes in garden or fields
- watching the weather and experiencing it
- investigating the local landscape and using elemental vocabulary to describe it
- using songs and poems to explore the wonder of the world
- begin to think about environmental concerns regarding water, waste, litter
- looking after a garden, planting, growing and tending

Skills

The skills that are developed by bringing the outside environment into the classroom are generic and should form part of good practice from the Foundation Stage onwards. These are:

- Observation – assist children to look carefully at what they see and taking time to do so
- Listening – combined with observation and in listening to others
- Talking – asking questions, debating, making statements, exchanging points of view which links in with listening skills
- Enquiry – formulating and asking questions with peers and adults
- Socialisation – co-operating and working with others in examining the environment
- Recording – finding ways to record what has been experienced

Conclusion

To become better citizens and be more environmentally aware, children need to be enabled to expand their personal geographies beyond the home to their neighbourhood and its connection with the wider world. The activities described in this chapter will show the way, and are suitable for children of any age. Safety concerns associated with taking children out of the school or nursery premises must be thoroughly planned. And it is important that practitioners consider their planning, teaching and learning in the context of what the world outside the classroom offers which will enhance children's learning. Children have a sense of the world around them from an early age so pre-school and school settings should be offering a natural step forward in children's understanding, rather than a leap into the unknown.

4

Using the built environment to generate musical composition

Jonathan Barnes

Introduction

Helping young people create satisfying patterns and arrangements with sound can be amongst the most enjoyable of teaching experiences. But most teachers avoid it. Classroom teachers often lack the confidence to tackle musical composition, because they feel inadequately trained and unskilled. This chapter is for these teachers! It suggests some easy and non-specialist ways of using buildings as the starting point for musical composition. It offers a simple framework to support and help progress children's compositions. No musical ability or experience is needed to make creative use of the ideas in this chapter.

Composition dominates the music National Curriculum (DfES/QCA, 1999), yet it is probably the least common aspect of music practised in primary schools (Philpott and Plummeridge, 2001; Grainger, Barnes and Scoffham, 2006). The National Curriculum (NC) and Curriculum Guidance for the Foundation Stage (CGFS) require teachers from the Early Years on to support children's experiments in organising sound and ensure progression towards pleasing, complex and characterful compositions.

'Music is frozen architecture', suggested the poet Goethe. Musicians have always responded to and influenced buildings of all kinds. Cathedrals, palaces and even some smaller homes have been built with the music which would happen within them in mind. Modern Greek composer and engineer, Xenakis, uses buildings as inspiration but also famously provided a musical score as the basis of architectural designs by Le Corbusier in Brussels. Buildings can help us understand music-making more fully. Materials in the school building can be used to examine the idea of musical timbre for example. Even the simplest architectural patterns in the classroom can be used to plan, explain and experiment with musical structure. Brickwork, railings, pathways and street furniture can all be used to help children understand and play with tempo, dynamics and texture. Silhouettes and skylines can become prompts for engaging work concerned with pitch. And the repeated patterns of walling, decoration, fenestration and whole building design may help us consider silence and duration. By the end of the chapter you will be able to use any building to inspire complex and sophisticated composition by children, whether in groups or individually.

Any interior or exterior environment can be the starting point for musical composition. The fine detail, novelty value and unique characteristics of individual places, usually beyond the classroom, can help make music more concrete, memorable and understandable to both teachers and children. More subtle characteristics of profile, decoration or plan might be used to inspire musical expressions which could include asymmetry, discord, surprise, sequence or unity. Many successful buildings conform to more classical restrictions which apply equally to music and architecture: symmetry, structure, texture, pattern, repetition, balance and harmony. Such architectural qualities in the built environment may be used to generate musical patterns, contrasts and structures which are equally satisfying.

Using the built environment as a learning resource is important because the buildings in which we live and which surround us are part of the world to which the child can truly feel they belong. Whether children are new to Britain or from families who have been here for generations, buildings represent their present culture, to which they have rights and responsibilities. Buildings are seen by people from all backgrounds as significant influences on well-being. The best are worth caring about and preserving (DCMS, 2001; Waterfield, 2004). As real and relevant parts of our world, buildings provide instant and motivating links across the curriculum.

Materials and timbre

Timbre means the quality of sound in music. Building materials can help children understand that sounds can have different qualities. Start inside. Look around your classroom. How many materials can you list? Wood, glass, plaster, metal, wire, plastic, brass, aluminium, iron, fabric, carpeting and paper will be in evidence in almost every classroom. Each material has distinctive qualities which our senses can discern and describe. The sense of touch will easily distinguish the cool of glass from the relative warmth of plastic. Most children will quickly tell wood from metal, or aluminium from iron. Imagine if we could not touch glass and plaster, how might we express their differences using only sound to help us? What sound could we make to express the smooth, shiny, brittle qualities of glass? What instruments could we choose to evoke the cold, rough and heavy feel of iron?

Figure 1: A paned window

Composing Frame: paned window

GLASS	PAINTED WOOD	GLASS
Scraaaaped cymbal	multiple hits on wood block	Scraaaaped cymbal

Ask your class to do a simple audit of materials in class. In groups of five or six, they are asked to make sounds which for them express the differences between the two materials. For example, express in sound the patterns of the classroom window from top to bottom, or the polystyrene tiles and reflective light fittings on the classroom ceiling from front to back.

Figure 2: Classroom ceiling

Composing Frame: classroom ceiling

POLYSTYRENE *Eg Ruffled plastic bag.*	POLYSTYRENE *Ruffled plastic bag*	POLYSTYRENE *Ruffled plastic bag*	SQUARED SHINY LIGHTS *Four scrapes on triangle*
POLYSTYRENE *Ruffled plastic bag*	POLYSTYRENE *Ruffled plastic bag*	SQUARED SHINY LIGHTS *Four scrapes on triangle*	POLYSTYRENE *Ruffled plastic bag*
POLYSTYRENE *Ruffled plastic bag*	SQUARED SHINY LIGHTS *Four scrapes on triangle*	POLYSTYRENE *Ruffled plastic bag*	POLYSTYRENE *Ruffled plastic bag*
SQUARED SHINY LIGHTS *Four scrapes on triangle*	POLYSTYRENE *Ruffled plastic bag*	POLYSTYRENE *Ruffled plastic bag*	POLYSTYRENE *Ruffled plastic bag*

Take children outside so they can make similar connections between materials and sound in the built and natural environment of the playground. This will extend the thinking and connection-making possibilities of the activity and give more scope for children to make their own creative links. The advantages of thinking about timbre in this way are that:

- there can be no absolutely wrong answers, so long as a child or group can think about and justify their choice
- the use of familiar varied materials will remind children that timbres need to be very distinct from each other to be audible
- an instant link is made between musical sound and the real world

Here are three more advanced examples of visual sources for sound ideas, chosen by Year One children when they visited a castle.

Figure 3a, b, and c: Floor boards, a brick wall and a galletted stonewall

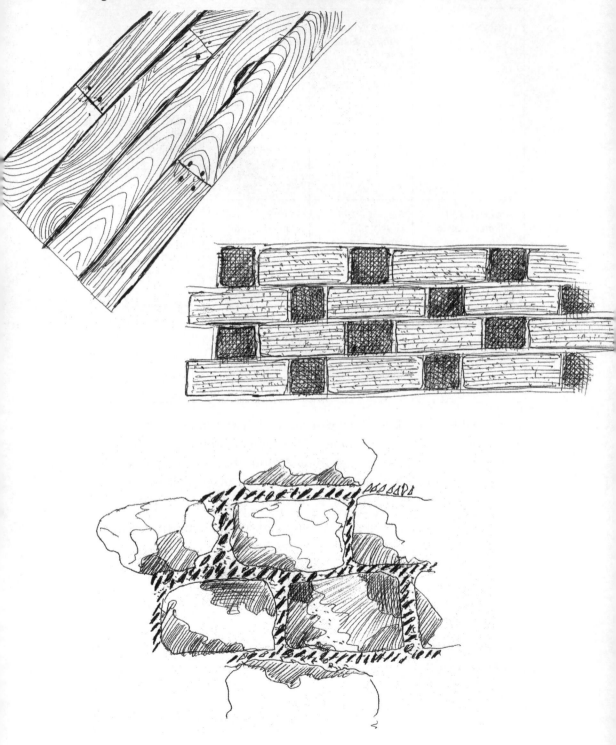

- Floor boards. Children chose to represent this on wood block and a 'slap stick' which crashed every time they 'read' the gap between floor boards

- A brick wall. Children chose to show this simple pattern by making short and long sounds by striking claves together

- A 'galletted' stone wall pattern. The pattern of tiny flakes of flint surrounding big blocks of stone was interpreted as slow bass drum notes, each surrounded by shaker sounds. Some children wanted yet another sound for the cement holding them all together and Nikki suggested sandpaper blocks

Built structures and musical structures

Look at any building near you. It is usually a collection of fairly simple shapes. Most buildings are constructed from a series of rectangles of different scales and proportions; the occasional square, circle, semicircle or triangle may be thrown in for interest. The majority of buildings have at least some symmetry and this makes them excellent stimuli for musical structures. We can go beyond that simple idea and read a building like a huge musical score. The dots and squiggles on a musical score are just symbols and the widows, bricks, chimney stacks and satellite dishes on a building can be interpreted as symbols too.

Read the building below (Figure 4) from left to right and use it as a composition frame. Tap out or imagine the musical patterns the ground floor

Figure 4: Eighteenth century house with five bays and a pediment in the middle of the first floor

suggests to you. Make two rapid taps for each window and separate them by the sound of your palms rubbing together to represent the brick wall. Now do the same with the first floor.

What are the differences? If a friend clapped out the patterns of the ground floor whilst you tapped out the first floor, at which points would you be clapping together?

The advantages of using a complete building as a massive musical score are:

- it can be approached at any level of complexity from a basic to a highly detailed reading and therefore provides its own differentiation
- it draws sonic attention to symmetry and other repeated features in a way which will engage those with musical intelligence (Gardner, 1999a).

On a castle visit a Year Two class used a cross section of the whole site to give a clear sense of structure to their castle music. Try to read these buildings in a similar way. Then try doing the same with a building near you.

Use these two drawings as composition frames:

Figures 5a and 5b: A bungalow and a castle

Tempo, dynamics and texture in the playground

Tempo relates to the speed, **dynamics** to the loudness or softness and **texture** to the number of different voices, layers or sound sources in music. Buildings and the 'street furniture' which surrounds them can help us understand these musical terms in practical and concrete ways. In building terms tempo might be represented by the number of repeated window patterns in a wall or posts in a fence (the more windows or posts the faster the tempo). The fences which surround many school playgrounds can help children understand tempo. Railings may be played by running a wooden stick against them while walking along them. The tempo would increase if someone ran while holding the stick against the fence. If someone sauntered slowly but regularly with their stick along the fence, the tempo would be slow. The fence remains the same but the tempo changes from *Andante* (a walking pace) to *Allegro* (a running pace) to *Largo* (a slow pace). With permission granted, metal railings can make good musical instruments to accompany outside performances themselves, but for class performances mimicking the sound of the fence with woodblocks or triangle will remind children of the importance of maintaining a regular tempo.

The changing heights of the building and outbuildings might be used to help children understand dynamics (the higher parts being louder). Look at the skyline from your classroom or stand outside the school and draw its silhouette. Use a silhouette drawing as an indicator of loudness and softness whilst the children make the sound shhhhh! Do the same using metal, wood or skin instruments.

shhhhhhhhhh**hh**hhhhhhhhhh – for a one-gabled building for example.

shhhh**hhhhh**hh **hhhh**hh**hh**hhhh **hhhhh**hh**hh**hhhh – for three gables.

s	hh	hh	h
s			h
s			h

Dynamic changes may also be prompted by changes in colour or texture or shadow on or in a building. One group of children made scary castle music using only dynamics and a host of metallic sounds. The sounds got louder and softer according to the contrasts of light and shade in the castle walls. Another group turned their classroom view of the silhouette of the city skyline into a pattern of light and shade which they expressed in the dynamics of their music. The darker high rise buildings were expressed as loud and metallic sounds of differing duration. The light sky between was expressed by the soft and continuous shakers whose sound was only revealed when the metallic instruments stopped.

Figure 6: A high rise silhouette

Texture might be decided by the number of floors – two floors and a pitched roof making a trio of contrasting sounds. Using the same idea and including earth, bushes, trees, ground floor and flat roof might suggest a continuous pedal note (the earth) with interludes of rattling sound (bushes) against a wall of unbroken xylophone sound. The whole composition might be capped by a high pitched recorder drone to represent the flat roof. The detail of texture can be as simple or complex as children make it. Thus a nearby building might be turned into music as follows:

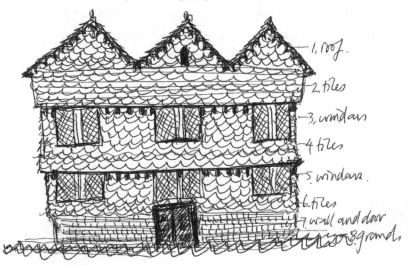

Figure 7: A tiled building

42

Shhhhh**h**hhhh Shhhhh**h**hhhh Shhhhh**h**hhhh [roof]

Shaker: shakeashakeashakeashakeashakeashakeashakeashakeasha [tiles]

Drum: bang bang   bang bang   bang bang   [windows]

Bells: tingalingtingalingtingalingtingalingtingalingtingalingtingaling   [tiles]

Drum: bang bang   bang bang   bang bang   [windows]

Bells: alingtingalingtingalingtingalingtingalingtingalingtingaling   [tiles]

Claves   tap tap tap tap tap BANG BANG tap tap tap tap tap   [wall and door]

Voices: hummmmmmmmmmmmmmmmmmmmmmmmmmmmmmmmmmmmm [ground]

Texture may also be found by looking down. The pathways in schools and other public places are often very varied. A short texture walk will reveal this. Paving stones, manhole covers, tarmac repairs, decorative brickwork pavements, pebbles, gravel and earth with autumn leaves all make different sounds under the feet. Using such found instruments to make music should be encouraged. Children can also represent their journey with musical instruments back in class and make a sound map of their journey along the different textures of pathway.

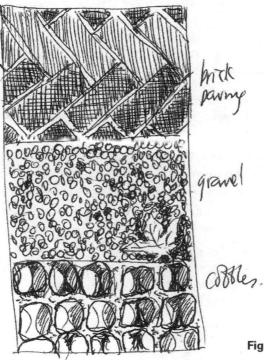

brick paving

gravel

cobbles.

Figure 8: Three pathway textures

Pitch – the long view

Just as silhouette can be used to think about dynamics, the profile of a building or street can also be the starting point for work on pitch – the highs and lows of musical sound. Young children could start with taking three steps and singing one note higher as we climb up each step. Small tunes can be picked out and recorded on a classroom displays using this simple link with real highs and lows.

Figure 9: Doh Re Me steps

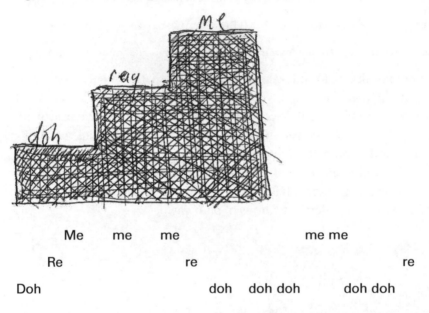

```
      Me    me    me              me me

   Re              re                    re

Doh                 doh  doh doh    doh doh
```

Children could be taken to a high point where they can take in a distant view to see multiple changes of level. One group used the ruins of an old abbey to guide them in making up their own multi-layered music. The high rugged walls of the north wall of the abbey became the main tune and were sung in plainsong fashion to *ahhhhh*. The seven arched windows became seven gentle rising and falling scales. The scales were sung simultaneously by a small sub group. Loud bursts of percussion placed between the scale windows marked the buttresses, and the grassy floor was represented by a long low sound on the gong. The same visit prompted a minimalist rendering of a brick wall with six instruments playing an identical pattern, each deliberately slightly out of time with the others.

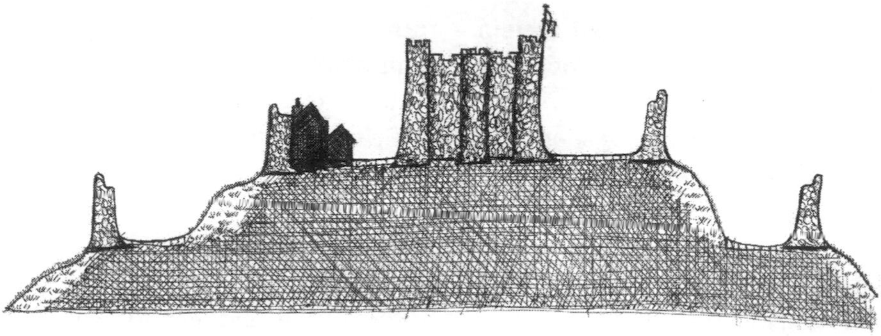

Figure 10: Cross section of Dover Castle

Figure 11: Archway

Architecture as frozen music – sound, silence and duration

Silence is as crucial to music as are the empty spaces between columns to the understanding and appreciation of Gothic architecture. Helping children enjoy the magic of silence is a significant aspect of satisfying music making. First, it is useful to teach children that music needs silence to signify its beginning and end. 'It's not me who wants you to be very, very quiet... it's the music,' one teacher used to say. Responding with silence when the baton is lifted or a conductor stands ready, is a simple discipline to teach, but does not usually happen automatically and needs practising with role play and frequent reminders. Playing with silence by leaving words out of well known songs is a good way of developing an understanding of silence and also teaching pulse. Silence might be more deeply understood through representing spaces in a building – gaps in fences, arches, doors, merlons in a castle wall or the sky between chimney pots – with an absence of sound.

Apparent silence may also be a good musical starting point. Children often think there is silence when no one is talking, but a sound trail around the school will remind them of the contrasting sonic atmospheres in this familiar place. It will also develop their listening skills. Find five or six contrasting sound worlds on the school site – perhaps the secretary's office, the playground at playtime, the quiet area, the gate near the street and the school hall – when no one is there. Take children around in small groups to record the sounds in each of these places either in words or on electronic recording devices. In class, each group uses musical instruments to represent the sound in their place. As a performance, recreate the journey by uses to represent the sound in their place a map to prompt responses from each group in turn, linking each composition by a 'shhhhhh' of white noise.

Buildings affect sounds made in or near them. Sound may be amplified, it may echo, it may be muffled or deadened by the space it is made in. Using buildings as extensions of musical instruments is an ancient practice. Classical, Romanesque and Gothic monuments were designed to make wonderful effects with sound as well as impress the eyes and lift the spirit. It is possible that the sound effects made in caves – perhaps the first homes for humans – were used to add mystery and power to the human voice. The simplest definition of music is, 'deliberately organised sound', so music can be made simply by opening and shutting a window four times and listening to the differences in sound when the window is open or closed. Composer John Cage experimented with this concept of music in his famous '*4 minutes 33 seconds*' composition which consists of three movements of total silence.

One group of six year olds enjoyed making a 'sound plan' of their school building during a science lesson. They tried to work out how long they could make a single shout, 'Hey!' last in different places:

- *the hall*
- *the corridor*
- *the playground*
- *near the terrace of houses at the back of the school.*

They loved debating why the sound in the playground near the houses lasted the longest, but the echoes against the many brick walls made them think of some exciting musical ideas too. They composed a piece of music called 'Hey', simply comprising of different ways the utterance 'hey' could sound.

Duration in music clearly has something to do with time. In music the term is generally used to describe the different ways in which time can be broken up by bursts of sound and silence. Duration is also used to describe the way in which musical time is parcelled up into groups or 3s, 4s or 2s. Duration can be more easily illustrated in the various repeating patterns which combine together to make the whole building. Look at a building near you to see how many repeating patterns there are. Each pattern has a different implied duration within it; small repeating patterns imply rapid beat and high numbered groupings,1,2,3,4,5,6,7,8; 1,2,3,4,5, 6,7,8. Large repeating patterns may suggest more ponderous rhythms and lower groupings of sounds 1- and 2- and 1- and 2- .

Figure 12: Drawing of view from office window

47

As I look outside my office window I see some patterns on the building opposite;

- *The regularly spaced pairs of windows give a steady sense of two beat pulse to the building this could be represented 1,2-1,2-1,2-1,2*

- *The brick pattern of the walls is very busy and provides a 'dot-dash' background rhythm which could be simultaneously expressed .-.-.-.-.-.-.-.-*

- *Pairs of chimney stacks strongly punctuate the fast repeated rhythms of the roof and could be represented by one beat crashes on a cymbal at the beginning and end of the piece.*

- *The roof itself is capped by a delicate, complex repeated zig- zag pattern of tiles which could be heard as shakers repeating a demi semiquaver rhythm and the ridge tiles as a semiquaver rhythm*

- *The roof is finished off at each end with a finial like a full stop – a triangle ring just before the cymbal*

Bigger compositions

Each of the ideas so far presented is simple but could be developed into pieces of minimalist music. The built environment near the school can also help with the invention of more multifaceted and longer lasting musical ideas. Composite and challenging pieces can be composed in collaborative groups and in this way creative possibilities multiply and the product improves (see John-Steiner, 2000). Here are a few ideas for group compositions:

- Each group takes a single shop in a shopping street and portrays its character/function/materials/style in music

- Each day the weather outside is the subject of a group composition which is recorded or written down in simple graphic notation. A week's weather is represented in five linked performances on Friday afternoon

- Five groups are given a challenge to compose a piece representing a row of houses in the nearest street. Each piece is to last a set number of seconds and must use the same instruments and the same 4/4 time, but each group is free to invent their own music with these restricted materials

▪ Groups are given different aspects of a building or room: walls, roof, ceiling, windows, doors, fittings or decoration. Each group prepares its composition based on key features of their part and then a whole class decision is made on how to assemble the pieces into a whole composition.

▪ Groups of five or six children go with a helper to different parts of the school or different streets nearby. They record the colours they encounter on a tick sheet – doors, flowers, building materials etc. Using a canned music ICT programme such as Dance EJay or sounds captured on a microphone, each colour is represented by a musical or found sound. Six red doors in the street might be represented, for example, by six bursts of a pre-recorded percussion sound. Two orange doors become two bursts of recorded keyboard music and black might be represented by a recorded clip of a child calling, 'hellooo!!'

red	Orange	Black	white	green	yellow	brown
✔✔✔✔✔✔	✔✔	✔	✔✔✔	✔✔	✔	✔✔✔

▪ When numbers of different but related pieces are composed in a class, it is a good idea to string them together around a repeated theme, making what is known as a *Rondo*. A, B, C and D may for example be different group musical responses to four different types of shop. The pre-recorded rondo theme (R) is played between each piece and gives the composition form and structure.

Composition Frame: A rondo

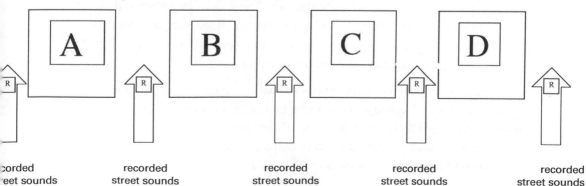

| recorded street sounds | recorded street sounds | recorded street sounds | recorded street sounds | recorded street sounds |

Presenting and performing

Composing with young children in sound is generally not just a matter of letting them express themselves freely. There are times when such free play with sound is valuable for understanding sound and its possibilities – indeed the fact that we *play* music is a reminder of the essentially playful nature of music making. Total freedom however, rarely results in inclusive experience, progression or any sense of musical challenge for the great majority of children. Paradoxically, creativity is most often stimulated by boundaries and restrictions (Nachmanovitch, 1990). Music is rightly called a discipline because at least at first it has rules and conventions and its language represents the combined wisdom and creativity of many ages, whatever our culture. Psychologists argue that our minds are genetically prepared to receive musical rules like tempo, duration, dynamics or pitch (Gardner, 1999a). The elements of music represent the kinds of restrictions all cultures impose on sound to make it into music (Gardner, 1999b).

In a recent lesson children were given a sheet of newspaper each as an instrument, a time restriction of thirty seconds and the instruction to compose a repeated, rhythmic pattern with a surprise. This may have been a stringent set of restrictions, but the children repeatedly came up with inventive and engaging ways to meet the challenge. It is for the teacher to provide the knowledge of the discipline so that such creative responses can be set free. Guy Claxton (1997) reminds us that 'Creativity favours not just a relaxed mind, but also one that is well- but not over in-formed'.

Research (Barnes and Shirley, 2005) has shown that open ended and cross curricular work is highly motivating to both student teachers and children. But if standards are to be raised and fuller participation in the curriculum ensured, more than simple enthusiasm is needed. Children need to be taught some knowledge and then quickly given opportunities to use it in real situations. Teachers who use the excitement of working beyond the classroom in real and stimulating environments have two key responsibilities: one is for the children's safety and security, the other is to promote deep, lasting and transferable learning.

Learning can be generated in a number of ways. First through genuine engagement, second through teaching which is seen to be relevant and meaningful, third through application of new knowledge, fourth through the comments and responses of peers and respected mentors – and lastly through performance. Presentation of 'work in progress' during musical composition was highlighted as a central process of the arts by the Arts Council in its seminal *Arts 5-16* report in 1990. If children working on musical compositions can feel safe in presenting their developing ideas to peers and if they can feel assured of positive and helpful feedback then the learning opportunities multiply. An atmosphere of trust, serious but playful experimentation, questioning, speculation, link-making and respect for the views and ideas of children is crucial to this atmosphere. It is the teacher's role to construct it.

5

Inner city spaces

Gina Donaldson

Introduction

What do inner city spaces offer for teachers to support and challenge children's mathematical learning? A look round any city reveals numerous obvious opportunities for mathematical learning. Shop displays provide real life use of money, with 3 for 2 offers and sale discounts; roads have speed limits and petrol stations advertise petrol for so much a litre. This chapter explores some of the less obvious but mathematically rich opportunities in inner cities. But first it dicusses the idea that using children's surroundings can provide a context which supports their learning.

Nunes, Schliemann and Caraher (1993) found that working class children in Brazil tend to perform poorly in mathematics in school, they often participate in selling items in street markets or on street corners, which requires quite complex mathematical calculations. Five young children identified by the researchers as street vendors were recorded as being able to complete calculations for several purchases.

> Interviewer: I'm going to take four coconuts (at Cr$35.00 each). How much is that?
>
> Child: Three will be 105, plus 30, that's 135... one coconut is 35... that is...140.
>
> (Nunes and Bryant, 1997, p106)

These children were asked whether they would be willing to solve some other problems later on and all agreed. So a few days later the researchers returned and gave them school type problems – both word problems and context free calculations – which required the same mathematical calculations as the original problems involved in the purchases. They found that although these children could calculate accurately in the context of the selling, they did less well in a school-based context.

> In the second interview, the same child solved 35 X 4 by writing the numbers down, one on the first line and the second one underneath, and explained the process out loud: '4 times 5, 20, carry the 2; 2 plus 3 is 5, times 4 is 20.' He obtained 200 as the result. (Nunes and Bryant, 1997, p106)

Ninety eight percent of the calculations for the purchases were correct, 74% of the word problems and 37% of the calculations presented without any context were answered correctly. Nunes found that the children calculating as part of their selling in a street market tended to use oral methods, speaking aloud as they counted up and down. The school type problems tended to be solved with written methods that were often poorly remembered.

Why should children be able to solve problems accurately in a real life setting but not in a school context? Atkinson (1992) and Hughes (1986) suggest that mathematics needs to make human sense to children. It should matter, have a reason and purpose. This motivates and engages children. A problem in a meaningful and familiar setting allows children to calculate in ways they use comfortably out of school, rather than by traditionally established school methods. The real life context empowers them to use their own methods of calculation. These may be intuitive and idiosyncratic, but are then open to the teacher for assessment and refinement. The skills of estimation and approximation matter as real life skills, especially when money or time, for example, are concerned. In school exercises, estimation and approximation rarely matter. This is often evident from the way children approach exercises where they are asked to estimate and then measure items drawn on a worksheet or in a textbook.

When children are working as part of the family business, or trying to set the DVD recorder to record a TV programme, accuracy matters. Real life and familiar contexts allow children to manipulate mathematical ideas in their minds. Even if the ideas are not concretely represented or cannot be seen, they can be imagined. This is the strength of using the immediate environment of children. In the Netherlands, the policy is to begin a mathematical topic with a realistic problem which allows ideas to be imagined by children (Thompson, 1999). Problems are carefully chosen to offer a source for particular mathematical ideas, and then provide a structure for mathematical learning. This is an alternative model to the one often used in the UK, where skills are taught and then typically applied to real life problems only at the end of a topic.

We know that young children's first learning of mathematical ideas is in real life contexts. Many writers such as Pound (1999), Montague Smith (1997), Worthington and Carruthers (2003) document how children negotiate the meaning of mathematical ideas and vocabulary through activities such as laying the table, counting for hide and seek, playing with stacking cups and construction materials. In contexts which are natural, young children are secure and stimulated to make mathematical sense of their world. Merttens (1999) contrasts this sort of learning at home with learning at school. At home children ask questions and learn in areas they find interesting. At school the curriculum is set, and the teacher is the questioner. The time spent on a task is different too. At home, the pace is usually set by the child. At school, the timetable can mean that activities are left unfinished and therefore not fully understood.

So it seems that children's natural environment might be the best starting point for learning. This is a feature of learning in many Early Years' settings, with the Curriculum Guidance for the Foundation Stage (DfEE/QCA, 2000, p70) affirming that 'Children's mathematical development arises out of daily experiences in a rich and interesting environment'. However, some research suggests that older children find learning in a real life context difficult. Selter (1999) found that older children misunderstood word problems which were designed to be set in a 'real life' context. They were given the problem: 'There are 26 sheep and 10 goats on a ship. How old is the captain?' 80% of the children gave an incorrect answer showing that they used the numbers in the problem inappropriately to give an answer of 36 years old. Arguably, the problem itself is not in a context which relates to the real life of many children. However, the research suggests that children can learn that mathematics is not about real life, and that the answers to problems do not have to make sense.

Furthermore, Nunes, Schliemann and Caraher's (1993) research in Brazil suggested that when children do learn in real life situations, they cannot easily transfer this learning to school based situations. There seems to be a gap between mathematical thinking at home and at school.

Worthington and Carruthers (2003) suggest that teachers should not see the learning which takes place in the home and community as just a starting point for children's learning of mathematics at school, but should make constant references relating learning at home and in the community to learning at school. Learning thus becomes meaningful, and children see mathematics not as simply abstract ideas and equations but as something useful in life, which matters and is fascinating for its own sake too. The environment is therefore more than a starting point for Early Years' education: it is a constant source of stimulating and supporting contexts for ongoing learning. Real contexts might not always be immediately visible to children, but digital photographs, perhaps on an Interactive White Board, of sites they know, will allow them to imagine and therefore manipulate and explore with mental images. Realistic problems set in commercially published textbooks or worksheets cannot hope to do this as effectively.

Let's look at specific aspects of inner city life to identify how they might be used to stimulate and support children's mathematical learning. More ideas are listed at the end of the chapter.

Number Lines

Identify a series of identical objects arranged closely and regularly along a city street, like lamp posts or railings. Take a digital photo of them and ask the children to count them with you. This can be reinforced from the classroom window, as a homework activity or during a trip out of school. Extend the objects into a number line. Use the photo or draw the lamp-posts on the whiteboard, labelling each one 1, 2, 3... Count forwards and backwards. If you are at post 2, how many posts would you pass to get to past 10? Use the posts as a context for counting on and back from any given number, extending into the empty number line and then adding zero. In the Netherlands a similar problem using posts across a beach develops a model for solving number line problems, which then becomes a model of the number line.

Figure 1: Posts can be used as a number line.

Younger children can use a familiar set of steps to explore number line ideas. Let children count the steps – on a railway bridge, car park, subway or in a shopping mall during a trip out of school. Use a digital photo of the steps to count them in the classroom and label each one. Recreate them with a small toy and a set of blocks. Count forwards as the toy ascends and backwards as the toy descends. Extend the children's understanding of the number sequence through questions such as: Which step is one higher than step 3? Starting on step 2 how many steps to get to step 6?

A lift in a high rise office block or block of flats can be used as a vertical number line. Number lines arranged vertically provide a strong image for greater than and lesser than. A hypothetical building might have a basement, extending the idea to include negative numbers, whilst thinking about buildings with lifts will aid the children's ability to imagine.

Shape

A shape trail around an inner city area presents opportunities for naming shape and discussing properties such as number of sides or vertices, angle, symmetry and tessellation. This can be extended back in the classroom with digital photographs. Young children can use viewfinders of various shapes, made from a piece of card with a triangular, circular, or rectangular hole in it, to explore views through classroom windows or close details of paving slabs or brickwork. Tessellation patterns can stem from careful observation of brick and paving slab patterns. Again, digital photographs, particularly on interactive white boards, and rubbings can extend the opportunities for learning back in the classroom over several lessons.

On a row of terraced houses or flats and shops try to spot examples of translation of shapes. Semi detached houses might offer examples of reflections of shapes. There may also be examples of translations, rotations and reflections in roof tile, pavement slabs and edgings and on places of worship. Recreate these using tracing paper.

Municipal gardens are often arranged symmetrically. They can be identified during class walks and then photographed for use in the classroom. Ask the children to identify the line or lines of symmetry, or the order of rotational symmetry. Cover up part of the display and ask them to describe the rest of it. A catalogue from a garden centre or supermarket would show children which bulbs or bedding plants are available. Ask them to use these to design a symmetrical garden or border.

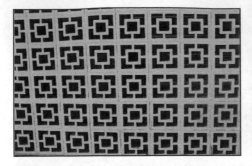

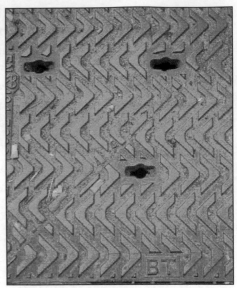

Above: Figure 2: Shape patterns in a brick wall

Right: Figure 3: Shapes on a manhole cover

Pattern

Try to identify repeating patterns of shapes. For example, railings may be formed from one large railing, followed by four smaller ones, one large, four small... These can be used to discuss simple ideas of ratio and multiplication patterns. If you draw part of the railings on the board, can the children identify what would come next? If you made a fence with 10 large railings, how many small railings would you need to go inbetween the larger ones and keep to the pattern?

Large	Small
2	4
3	8
4	12
5	16
6	20

By drawing up the table shown, older children might be able to state a general rule which lets them work out how many small railings are needed for a certain number of large railings – in this case (L-1) x 4.

Sets of windows in tall building can provide strong visual images of multiplication patterns and work on factors. If windows have 4 small panes of glass, how many small panes of glass are there in 8 windows? If a block of flats has 6 storeys, with 8 windows on each storey, how many windows are there altogether? If a block of flats has 6 windows on each floor and 24 windows altogether, how many storeys are there? Draw blocks of flats which have 36 windows. This could be one storey of 36 windows, 2 storeys of 18 windows, 3 storeys of 12 windows....Investigate and link to the factors of 36. Use multiplication to help count the bricks making a rectangular wall, or paving slabs along a pavement.

Figure 4: Patterns of railings

Figure 5: Windows on a building arranged in arrays

Angle

Navigating toy cars around representations of one way road systems in city centres or car parks allows children to use and negotiate the meaning of the language of angle. forwards, backwards, left, right, clockwise, anti clockwise, full, half and quarter turns. This can be consolidated by activities entailing children describing their route to school or between certain landmarks in the city. Parts of the city can be recreated in the classroom for a programmable toy to negotiate. If the classroom isn't spacious, choose a small area of the city such as the queuing system in the post office, bank or cinema.

Signposts offer opportunities for exploring static examples of angle. Use signposts to review the vocabulary of angle during the beginning of a lesson or to introduce a problem solving activity. Roundabouts often have quite complicated signposts and these will stretch the more able children.

Length and area

Use local maps to calculate problems of scale. Plan routes to well known places and look for the shortest possible routes.

Visit or study pictures of local car parks. Are the spaces all the same size? This should be based of the length and width of an average car. Can the children calculate this? How wide are the roadways in the car parks? Give the children a specific area of ground and ask them to design a car park with the most spaces possible. This will require work on scale.

Other possible mathematical activities in the city:

- Takeaway restaurants often offer free delivery in a five mile radius. Where can you live and still get free delivery?
- Free takeaway menus can be used for money activities
- Does travelling in twos halve the traffic jams at rush hour? How many cars can be seen carrying two or more people?
- Count how many vehicles can go through a green light
- Are % off offers always correct?
- Plan a trip using local public transport timetables
- Do television aerials and dishes on the tops of buildings all point in the same direction?
- Look for parallel lines in a picture of a high street or residential road. Scaffolding on a building offers many examples of parallel and perpendicular lines
- Set problems with time and money using a pay and display machine
- Make explicit links between the home, community and school mathematics by asking children to keep a mathematics diary. They should note when they use mathematics in their lives and discuss these occasions at school so that the links are clear.

Figure 6: A pay and display machine

Conclusion

Once a teacher's eyes are open to the potential of inner city spaces, the rich opportunities become apparent. This chapter has stressed the importance of building on Early Years' practice of using children's immediate experiences as a starting point for mathematical learning. The home and community provide a constant source of problem solving contexts which allow children to make sense of mathematical concepts, use and refine their intuitive strategies and explore mathematics itself. The outside is a resource for children's learning throughout their education, not only to motivate them and show them that mathematics is useful, but to scaffold their understanding. Frequent references during mathematics lessons to real situations, and the use of school mathematics in real life enable children to make connections. Being able to imagine and develop mental images for mathematics set in familiar contexts equips children to manipulate ideas and numbers with confidence.

6
Developing pedagogically appropriate practice
Jane Williams-Siegfredsen

A Scandinavian tradition

Depending upon who you ask, the forest and nature nursery tradition started in Norway, Sweden or Denmark – all stake a claim to being the originator. What can be said is that it is a Scandinavian tradition. In Denmark it started in the 1960s as good pedagogical practice to use nature and the outdoor environment with young children, giving them freedom and space to play and discover natural phenomena. By the 1980s it also made economic sense as a rapid increase in the numbers of working mothers and created more demand for child care places; by having outdoor groups the nurseries could offer more places.

Today, no two Early Years' settings use the outdoor environment in the same way. Practice and provision depend on where the settings are situated – in rural, semi-rural or urban areas – and on the people using them – educators, children and parents. There are nurseries situated in woodland, usually referred to as wood or nature nurseries. In these the natural surroundings provide the starting point for activities inside and outside for the whole or much of the day, every day, all year round. Sometimes things are discovered and investigated by the children and educators in the natural surroundings outdoors and other times things may be brought inside for investigation and discussion. Most of these wood and nature nurseries are small, with twenty to thirty children and four or five educators; a few are much larger with a hundred or more children.

Another common type of provision are nurseries that have 'wood groups' – groups of children and educators who go out for part of the week or the whole week to a woodland area, often by bus. These nurseries usually have a permanent or semi-permanent shelter in the wood. Wood groups in urban areas where woodland is too far away rent allotments in town and develop them into an outdoor environment.

Not all nurseries in Denmark are specific wood or nature nurseries, nor do all have wood groups. Many nurseries just use the outdoor area they have available, but even in these the children are outside for part of each day all year round.

The curriculum, competence and the outdoors

In the Early Years' curriculum in Denmark, emphasis is on nurturing children's social and emotional development, inter- and intra-personal. Formal pre-school teaching of children, in the traditional sense of classroom learning, is generally frowned upon by educators and parents alike. The central aim of the Danish Early Years' curriculum is to create a 'competent child' and regular access to the outdoors is seen as a key means to achieving this.

Competence, in terms of the Danish curriculum, represents the abilities – social, emotional and cognitive – and proficiencies that can be fostered and developed in children. A list of competences would include literacy, numeracy, logical thinking, physical education and a range of dispositions such as: to attend, concentrate, co-operate, reason, imagine possibilities and be inquisitive. The view is that it isn't enough to have 'knowledge' – to know how to read, write and add – alongside knowledge, children need the skills and competences to use the knowledge they have.

The curriculum for pre-school institutions in Denmark is less formally presented than in the UK, but every institution has to develop an institutional curriculum that covers six areas of learning:

- The child's all-round personal development
- Social development
- Language
- Body and movement
- Nature and natural phenomena
- Cultural expression and values

Within these areas are four learning processes: 'to be able', 'to experience', 'to enjoy' and 'to understand' (Hansen, 2003).

In order 'to be able' to develop physical skills children need opportunities to climb, jump, run, cycle etc and these processes include the sensory, bodily, social and intellectual competences that children develop through such opportunities. Children develop a positive self-image by using the outdoor environment because they can test themselves in the physical activities in which they participate. They develop important self-regulatory skills by learning to take turns and follow routines.

'To experience' in nature means that children can feel wonderment in the outdoors, joy and happiness, as well as experiencing the potentially frightening, in the knowledge that others around them are keeping them safe.

'To enjoy' means that children, through nature, take pleasure in sensory experiences – the smells, sounds, tastes and touch that being in an outdoor environment brings. Sitting round a fire, feeling its warmth on a cold day, listening to the trees rustling in the wind and tasting the pancakes made on the fire, all give enjoyment that is part of the learning process.

'To understand' means that the outdoor environment is the natural arena for children to learn about some of the mysteries of life – life-cycle processes, ethics and morals can be discussed by the educators and children in their natural context. Finding a dead animal, for example, raises many discussions on life and death, and the fascination the next day on discovering that the animal has disappeared or been partly eaten, deepens understanding of the forces of nature and gives children the chance to talk about their feelings – sympathy, fear etc.

These four learning processes are crucial if the child is to develop the skills and competences of being a whole person.

The careful balance between the curriculum, the activities and the educators' awareness of facilitating children's emerging skills and competences is the key to developing pedagogically appropriate practice. To develop pedagogically appropriate practice it is essential that the adults trained to work with young children are themselves competent and are disposed to be inquisitive and ready to take on challenges. They need to be creative, imaginative and resourceful and alert, informed and observant. In Denmark trained educators are called 'pedagogues', a term derived from the Greek *paidagogos*, a slave who took boys to school and on the way discussed the natural phenomena around them and helped the children develop a wonderment of the world.

The pedagogical training of educators combines the theoretical and the practical with the development of the educator's own self-awareness through physically and mentally challenging activities. A good educator is one who can point out interesting things to children, focusing their attention on the details of nature and natural phenomena. Communication is vital: the educator should talk to the children, explaining, questioning and discussing everything wherever and whenever possible. Educators also have to be prepared for the unexpected – the weather, or an unusual find. The best tenet is to expect the unknown, because unlike the indoor classroom which can be planned, the outdoor classroom is natural and ever-changing – we cannot control nature!

Challenge and risk

Much is written about risk and the fears of adults about the dangers of young children using real tools, playing freely outdoors and facing the risks or challenges the outdoor environment might present (Williams-Siegfredsen, 2005). Physical safety must certainly be taken seriously, but allowing children opportunities to assess risk for themselves avoids over-reliance on the control of others, which may prove more hazardous in the longer term. Children need to experience real-life materials at first hand and learn how to use them – tools, fire, trees etc – respectfully, efficiently and confidently. Accidents are more likely to occur if children only start using natural materials and tools at the age of eight or nine. Or take the activity of climbing for example: very young children generally only climb to a height they are comfortable with, a height that challenges but does not threaten them, such as clambering onto an upturned log. Success in learning to climb in small stages encourages children to gradually develop their confidence and competence to climb higher – and climb down again – safely.

Using real tools such as knives, axes, saws etc, in the same small stage approach also encourages children's confidence and competence safely. The pedagogically appropriate practice used to teach young children to use tools is this:

- first children watch the educator using real tools and the educator and children talk about the actions and why it is important to use the tools safely
- next the child uses the tools alongside the educator
- when the children have mastered using the tools and have shown the educator that they are using the tools confidently and safely, they begin to use them alone.

If we presuppose that children will harm themselves or others when using natural materials and tools we are disabling them. We make them feel unsure, frightened and incompetent – and therefore more likely to have an accident.

Although the health and safety regulations for child care institutions throughout Europe are the same, there are cultural differences between the attitudes, understandings and interpretations of practitioners and parents in Denmark and those in other European countries (Cameron, 2005). Most Danish local councils regularly conduct surveys of parents and practitioner values and thoughts about the activities and experiences provided by the council's child care institutions. A recent survey in Copenhagen's local council shows that parents and practitioners agree that the most important values that children need to develop are:

- self-worth
- independence
- consideration for others
- tolerance

And that the most important experiences children should have in institutions are:

- experiences of, and in, nature
- experiences with animals
- experience of peace and tranquillity (Copenhagen Council, 2003)

Parental involvement in nurseries and schools is high in Denmark; all establishments have committees of parents which meet regularly. Most preschool institutions have working weekends, two or three times a year, when the parents, the children and the educators spend the weekend tidying, cleaning, building and mending at the nursery. It is as much a social occasion as a working one and a time when all can get to know each other

in ways outside the usual roles and routines. And it gives children the chance to show their parents their favourite things and, importantly, be actively involved in the physical development and construction of the nursery.

Underlying all this is the importance of practitioners and parents working together and agreeing the activities and experiences that are important for children. Positive attitudes about children's experiences outdoors how they learn to take risks and face challenges in safe circumstances have to be developed collaboratively.

Just fresh air?

Why has using the outdoors as an everyday learning environment for children become popular in the past couple of decades? Is it just because it's a good place to let off steam? We know that exercise and fresh air are healthy and that children enjoy being outside during playtime and their free time, but is an outdoor environment really better for children to develop and learn in? Underpinning pedagogically appropriate practice is research that shows how exposing children to learning and playing in the fresh air is beneficial in many ways. Research in Sweden by Grahn *et al* (1997) has significantly influenced using the outdoor environment with children in educational institutions. It was one of the first to show that children who are outside for a large part of every day all year round are better developed socially and physically, use more complex and imaginative play, have better levels of concentration and are ill less often than children in traditional nurseries. The research showed dramatic differences between the children from the two nursery schools used in the study. One was a 'nature nursery' where the children were outside practically all day every day, the other a traditional town nursery where the children were out for short periods during the day. The study showed that:

- The children in the outdoor nursery had measurably better abilities in concentration. Using a form of the Attention Deficit Disorders Evaluation Scale (ADDES), the educators in the two nurseries observed the children over the one year period of the study. The data showed that the outdoor nursery children were more attentive, had better powers of memory, were less easily distracted and concentrated on activities for longer.

- The children in the outdoor nursery had better physical and motor development. Using the Eurofit test recommended by the European Council in 1993, tests were given to representative groups of children in each nursery. The data showed that the children from the outdoor nursery had better balance, agility and strength in their hands, arms and bodies.

- There were differences in types of play used by the children, the outdoor nursery children showed more varied and imaginative types of play, had more complex procedures and roles and seldom disturbed each others' games and activities. The children also spent longer on an activity, often continuing and developing the activity over periods of days.

- The children from the outdoor nursery were less often ill. Children's absences because of illness were compared – these children were absent 2.8% of the year compared to 8.0% in the traditional nursery.

The results of this research were widely disseminated and promoted a wider research interest in children and nature.

More recent research shows that physical activity is essential for our well being and that modern societal trends of people taking less exercise and the increase in sedentary occupations and hobbies all lead to health problems that affect us physically and psychologically. Every four years Copenhagen University undertakes a national survey of school children in Denmark. This indicates that on average children are becoming more obese, which may lead to health and economic problems for society as a whole in the near future. It has been shown that overweight children are more likely to become overweight adults and are therefore more likely to contract diseases such as type two diabetes, high blood pressure and heart disease.

Bente Karlund Pedersen, professor of internal medicine at Righospitalet and Copenhagen University, has researched the muscle hormone Interleukin 6, which keeps our bodies strong, healthy and slim, but also has an effect upon our brains, increasing learning and memory. Professor Pedersen has also measured and compared the length of the hamstring muscles of children in traditional and outdoor nurseries and found that the children in outdoor nurseries have longer hamstring muscles and that there is a close correlation between muscle development, the brain and social behaviour (Pedersen, 2005).

Swedish physician Britt-Louise Theglander has researched the connection between traditional methods of teaching indoors and learning methods outdoors. She concluded that children learn better outdoors because movement and activity are essential for their brain function (Theglander, 2001). She points out that it isn't enough that we learn – we need to remember also what we have learned. And we remember mostly the things that interest us, things that give us pleasure or pain – not physical pain but also pain from the possibility of danger. Theglander recommends that children who are in a learning situation should have movement every ten minutes to achieve optimum brain function in both learning and memory.

There is also evidence that learning outdoors stimulates language development (Herholdt, 2003). Children use more complex language and construct longer sentences outdoors. For one thing, the children outdoors are usually in pairs or groups, so interaction, together with learning first hand from real-life materials and experiences, significantly enhances their language development.

We learn most when we are motivated and our motivation has a good deal to do with how we feel in and about the learning environment we are in. Being happy in learning situations is about doing something that not only gives pleasure but also absorbs one's time in an enjoyable way and leads to deeper fulfilment. Csikszenthmihalyi (1992) calls this feeling of happiness 'being in flow'. The theory of 'flow' and learning through optimal experience is widely used in Denmark, especially in trying to understand what motivates and develops children's learning and competences. When we are 'in flow' our skills and competences are well matched to the challenges we face. The situation may test us but by using our skills and competences we can achieve our target. If the challenges are too great, we feel frustrated and anxious; if the challenges are too meagre for our abilities we become bored and easily distracted. Csikszenthmihalyi calls these three regions the 'flow' zone, the 'panic' zone and the 'drone' zone. Pedagogically appropriate practice will ensure that children are in their 'flow' zone to maximise their learning potential. This requires giving children clear goals so they know what needs to be done, and ensuring that they receive immediate feedback about their actions. To find the balance between challenges and children's skills, educators have to be observant and be aware of each child's abilities. In the outdoor environment the natural materials help children develop their skills in a realistic, hands-on manner and the environment provides the degree of challenge. Thus, with help and guidance from the educator, children can always find challenge in their 'flow' zone when they are outdoors .

A case to conclude with

Observations of young children in Denmark over the past nine years have noted many aspects of using the outdoor environment. One is in children's development of social competences. Because children play more co-operatively out of doors, a different hierarchy pertains, one in which each child brings their own skills to the group. Children seem more tolerant outdoors and more open to mixing with children they don't mix with indoors. It is interesting to observe the different ways children engage with each other and resolve conflicts outdoors as opposed to indoors. One observation involved going out on a daily walk through the woods with the children and educators in a nature nursery. Most of the children were in groups, running, playing and talking. One little boy, Hans, was at the back alone, dragging his heels and going slower and slower, so I slowed down and walked with him. He told me he didn't want to talk because his best friends had left the nursery to start school and he missed them. Half way through the walk we stopped for a short break and two boys started to build a den out of pieces of wood and branches. Hans stood close by

watching them, but they didn't speak to each other. After a while Hans walked away and returned with a piece of wood and stood holding it close by the boys, still silent. After a bit one of the boys looked at Hans and said 'that's a great piece of wood for our den, come and put it on'. Within moments the three were playing together. At the end of the break they left the den, saying they would return to it the next day to continue their work. The three boys walked back together talking about their den and what other things they could do to it.

It was interesting that Hans didn't push himself onto the two boys but, by quietly observing what they were doing, he found a way to join them. It was clear also that the boys were impressed with the piece of wood Hans had found and valued his contribution. The educators watched it all but did not intrude, understanding Hans's predicament: on one hand he was missing his best friends but on the other he wanted to play with the other children, but needed time and space to find his own way to solve his dilemma. The outdoor environment gave him the space and peace to use his developing skills and competences of co-operating, reasoning and communicating, and the natural material – the piece of wood – acted as a bridge for him to communicate his needs to the boys without words. This kind of collaboration, showing fellowship and respect, is commonplace in the outdoor environment and illustrates the ability of children to grow and learn to their fullest in their uniquely experiential way through the joy of exploration and discovery in the natural environment.

Pedagogically appropriate practice is a careful balance, somewhere between art and science. It's rather like what Einstein meant when he said that imagination is more important than knowledge. Not that knowledge is unimportant, but rather that without imagination, knowledge cannot be used effectively or meaningfully. Educators need to be constantly mindful of their role as facilitators of children's learning and development.

7

'Making the best of what you've got': adopting and adapting the Forest School approach

Trisha Maynard

Introduction

In the last few years initiatives promoting the learning potential of woodland have been established in the UK. A number of these collaborate with the Forest Education Initiative (FEI). The FEI, launched in 1992, aims 'to increase young people's understanding and appreciation of the benefits of trees, woodlands and forests in our everyday lives' through a network of cluster groups. These groups generally work directly with schools, so providing children with the opportunity of learning in and about the natural environment.

FEI has become involved in Forest Schools, which has its roots in Scandinavia and which is closely associated with the Early Years' programme in Denmark. The concept of Forest School was brought to the UK in 1995 by staff from Bridgwater College, Somerset, who had visited Denmark on an exchange visit and were impressed by how much emphasis was placed on outdoor activities. Numerous Forest Schools have since been established and many of them are registered as FEI Forest Schools.

This chapter describes the practice of two Early Years' teachers who were inspired by Forest School ideas and adapted them to fit the settings in which they worked.

It considers:

- the teachers' initial understandings about Forest School
- the extent to which they felt that Forest School was appropriate for the children they worked with
- the modifications they made to the Forest School approach

Forest Schools in the UK

First, I describe the Forest School concept as established in the UK, focusing on its use with young children. Because there is little published research on this initiative, I analysed four Forest School websites: two that are not part of the FEI (Bridgwater College Forest School, Great Limber Forest School) and two that are (Oxfordshire Forest Schools and Shropshire Forest School).

Forest School, it appears, is promoted as being for everyone from age three upwards. Children attend the Forest School, which is normally held in a local woodland, for a half or whole day on a regular – preferably weekly – basis throughout the year whatever the weather. Sessions are led by qualified Forest School leaders and there is generally one adult for every four to six children. The websites accessed indicate that the Forest School approach is introduced gradually to young children. The Oxfordshire Forest Schools website, for example, notes that in the initial visits to the woodland, children are encouraged to explore the natural environment and take part in games such as '1, 2, 3 where are you?' (a form of Hide and Seek). As children become more comfortable in the outdoor environment they often initiate games and activities for themselves although, it is suggested that teachers should have a few ideas 'in their back pocket'. Later in the programme, when children have understood basic safety rules, they may be introduced to adult-size tools such as saws, loppers and penknives, which can be used for building shelters, making mallets, building a fire or whittling sticks for toasting marshmallows (Oxfordshire Forest School).

Aims

The websites accessed all indicate, although with different degrees of emphasis, that Forest School promotes the development of children's self-esteem and confidence. Forest School is also seen to promote independence (Bridgwater College and Great Limber), communication and social skills (Shropshire and Oxfordshire), teamwork and a positive disposition towards learning (Oxfordshire). Most aim to encourage children to appreciate, care for and respect the natural environment. Children 'follow'

(Oxfordshire and Shropshire) or can 'access' (Great Limber) their usual curriculum but do so outdoors and through a practical, hands-on and essentially child-led approach to learning. As well as being given time to explore and play in the natural environment, the children are provided with activities – small, achievable tasks – which may be tailored to meet their individual learning styles (Bridgwater College and Great Limber) and at which they are likely to succeed.

While the Forest Schools share many of the same aims, strategies and activities there appears to be a subtle difference of emphasis: the two projects not registered as FEI Forest Schools seem to foreground the enhancement of children's personal and social development, whereas the FEI Forest Schools see children's personal and social development as a desirable outcome of the way in which the statutory curriculum – and particularly, though not exclusively, environmental education – is taught in a natural, outdoor environment.

Having outlined the aims and approach of Forest School we turn now to the two teachers: Molly and Leanne.

The teachers
Molly
Molly has 28 children in her nursery class and is supported by one nursery nurse. The school is situated in the suburbs of a city in South Wales and has extensive grounds. These have been developed to include various yards, grassy slopes, a round house, a sensory garden, a willow tunnel, a bridge, a willow dome and a pond, as well as a small wooded area that is used for Forest School sessions. Molly describes herself as an 'outdoorsy' sort of person and so when she first heard about Forest School training, she applied (unsuccessfully) to go on the course. Last summer she attended a presentation about Forest School and this, she said, made her realise that she had to introduce this approach in her setting. She visited a school in England to spend a day with a teacher and Learning Support Assistant who were Forest School trained. Molly sees the Forest School approach as concerned with:

> ...learning about the forest and survival skills...building shelters, looking at wildlife and making children aware of the versatility of the natural environment. It's about developing physical independence, emotional independence. It's about handling tools correctly and being able to build shelters... things like that...

Molly said that although she found these ideas interesting she was unsure whether what she saw as the tight structure of Forest School and the focus on learning about the forest was entirely appropriate for very young children. Molly therefore adapted the approach to suit her setting:

> ...rather than restricting planning to learning about the forest I looked at all the areas of learning. As a starting point I made a note of all the activities I was going to try and do. I then decided that whichever of these I could do outside we would go and do in the forest – but using the resources that are down there. My approach is about learning in and through the forest environment.

Initially, Molly was concerned about how parents would respond to Forest School so sent letters home explaining what she intended to do and why. She also informed parents that although she would not take the children out in extreme conditions, they would generally go outside 'whatever the weather' so it was important that they came dressed appropriately. A few weeks into the programme Molly invited parents to attend a presentation on her version of Forest School activities. Six parents promptly offered to become helpers, so when Molly works outside she now has one adult for every three to four children. They take the children to the forest for one morning every week – an area about four times the size of an average classroom which has a variety of trees, shrubs and wildflowers. Molly described two of the activities she initially tried in the forest:

> We took ropes and tunnels and a groundsheet and together we constructed an obstacle course. We tied the ropes to the trees and hung the hoops and they'd climb though, over and under. On another session... it was raining and we were going to do Noah's ark for assembly. I had read them the story so we went into the forest and built a Noah's ark out of logs... I took loads of photographs and ...they loved to talk about it and I wrote down what they said and they drew pictures and we made books.

Molly noted that lately her approach had changed. She was now less concerned about planning sessions in advance; she felt more comfortable with 'letting the children do what they want to do'. While she still set up activities and invited the children 'to have a go', she noticed that they preferred to invent their own games. For example, several of the girls enjoyed 'cooking' using shells, leaves and twigs, one group of boys enjoyed fantasy play centred on dinosaurs while another group of boys preferred to climb trees. So instead of thinking about 'activities', Molly now tended to think more in terms of 'resources' the children might like to use to extend their play.

> I take buckets and spades down; we've got rucksacks and I take lots of things, string, scissors, bags, wet wipes. They know what's in the rucksack now so if they want things...

Her school was a designated 'eco school' and Forest School therefore 'fitted in with the whole ethos'. Molly described how:

> ...we used to have a parent preparing the fruit for snack time but now the nursery nurse does it and there's a bit of maths...share out the banana, share out the apples... and I make a point of whoever does the fruit takes the peelings outside to put them in the compost...and we have planting beds. Last week a mum came in to help them to plant potatoes and radishes and beans and we went round to the compost bin and she took the lid off and we got some compost and took it round in a bucket to do our planting...

What was important about this, Molly emphasised, was that she now implemented a holistic approach which integrated the ideas and activities of 'school', 'eco school', 'Forest School'.

Leanne

Leanne teaches a Year One class in a school on the outskirts of a city in South Wales. It too has fairly large grounds, mainly grass and a wildlife area that is currently used for Forest School sessions. This area consists of trees, mainly birch, and there is a little pond. A privet hedge makes a natural boundary. Leanne described the wildlife area as 'fairly small', saying: 'it's about working with what you've got... and making the best of what you've got'.

When interviewed, Leanne was just completing her Forest School training based on the Bridgwater College model. She believed that Forest School was essentially concerned with children's emotional learning and self esteem and focused on dealing with challenging behaviour: 'not so much curriculum based as personal and social...' Leanne's head teacher fully supported making greater use of the outdoor environment so agreed that a modified Forest School approach would be introduced into all seven Early Years' classes.

Leanne was aware that she needed to convince her colleagues of the benefit of this approach, however, and especially to win over the parents. So to alleviate anxieties about muddy clothes and as a statement of their commitment, the school bought waterproof outfits for all the children to wear when working outdoors. Leanne organised a presentation for parents on the Forest School approach. Anticipating that parents might be concerned about 'any loss of teaching time', she told them about some of the activities undertaken outside and explained how they related to areas of the curriculum. She told me:

> We went through the educational side of it first... we told parents we would still be *teaching* the children... it would just be through the outdoor environment. So I made a list of various things we would do for knowledge and understanding of the world... environmental issues, physical development... pulling the logs, moving things outside... and there was communication... and personal and social development and creative development – these were going to be the main areas we would focus on.

The parents were invited to have a look at the wildlife area. Regularly updated information and photographs of the children taking part in Forest School activities are displayed on Leanne's classroom window. As a result, four parents from the seven classes were keen to be trained as Forest School leaders. Leanne also considered the children's reactions to the new approach and planned a series of activities aimed to dispel any fears they might have. Leanne began by talking with the children about their experiences in different outdoor environments and how these made them feel. They discussed familiar fairy tales and how forests were often portrayed in them as scary places. Children were encouraged to talk about positive memories of being outside, such as going on picnics. When the children eventually went to the wildlife area they built a base camp of logs arranged around a central space which could later be used for a fire.

Leanne remarked that lately the way she thought about the Forest School sessions had changed. While she still incorporated the development of children's practical skills and tried to provide children with 'small, achievable tasks', she no longer planned Forest School activities as something separate from the rest of the curriculum. She explained:

> I used to plan Forest School activities totally as Forest School activities. But then I went on a course and someone said, it's far easier to go through your planning and highlight things in one colour that *can* be done outdoors and highlight things in a different colour that can be *adapted* to being able to be done outdoors. And I thought, that's what I should be doing.

Leanne reported that when they worked in the wildlife area she didn't take any classroom equipment with her but 'just tended to focus on what's there'. For example, 'the children had looked at the pond and had seen that it needed clearing so had got involved in that'. Children had also been involved in clearing up litter: Leanne commented that:

> ...the children were mortified that people had been dropping litter in their wildlife area. And then it took on a new aspect of recycling and the compost we started as well...so children have got an increased awareness of environmental issues from that. And if they now see people dropping litter they will say 'that's not right!'

She observed that when working outdoors she was more child-led in her approach even when she had no additional support. If her one adult helper was unavailable, the adult-child ratio was one to thirty. Leanne did not see this as 'a particular problem' although she noted that it that it meant she couldn't easily have in-depth conversations with individual children.

In future, Leanne said, she intended to introduce children to some of the skills she had learned about on her Forest School training course.

> I am looking forward to making a fire with the children and I never thought I would...and using the tools as well. At first, the teacher side of me was – safety issues. But the Forest School leader showed us how to use them and I can see it's safe.

Molly and Leanne's initial understanding about Forest School broadly reflected the aims and approaches described on the websites. Significantly though, while both teachers referred to children's personal and social development – and Molly also mentioned 'learning about the forest' – neither saw Forest School as being a way of teaching the normal curriculum in the outdoor environment.

The teachers' feelings about the suitability of Forest School for their children

Molly and Leanne both maintained that in principle they were very supportive of the Forest School approach. Leanne said she intended to introduce activities such as lighting fires and using adult tools at some stage. Molly was unsure whether such activities, and also what she saw as the tightly structured nature of Forest School, were appropriate for very young children. She indicated that for the children in her class, being provided with the opportunity to play in the outdoor environment itself satisfied the need for excitement and challenge (Bilton, 2002) and enhanced the development of confidence and self esteem (Stephenson, 2003).

That Molly and Leanne were concerned about introducing activities which could be perceived as risky was unsurprising in our litigious climate and in Leanne's case, the lack of adult support when working outside was an issue. Even so, it is worth remembering that attitudes towards young children experiencing fire and handling adult tools vary across times and cultures (see Rogoff, 2003) and that in line with the ideas of Rousseau, Danish kindergartens put the four elements – earth, air, fire and water – at the centre of children's experiences of their world (OECD, 2001: 26).

Modifications the teachers made to the Forest School approach

Admittedly, Molly and Leanne were fortunate to be located in settings with considerable outside space – this isn't the case for all practitioners. That said, what seemed to be important was not so much the size of the outdoor environment but that the topography and vegetation of the area used for Forest School activities made it appropriately diverse and challenging. Fjortoft (2004) has indicated that environmental features such as trees, shrubs, rocks, hollows and slopes are seen as affordances by children for different kinds of play – for example, trees the opportunity to climb and slopes the opportunity to roll or slide. It is likely, therefore, that each Early Years' setting will provoke and challenge children to engage in different forms of play as well as promoting different learning experiences.

Although Molly and Leanne were both excited by Forest School ideas, they found it difficult to make them work in practice. Rather than thinking about Forest School as something separate from or additional to children's day-to-day activities they both decided it was easier and more appropriate to incorporate the use of the outdoor environment into their normal curriculum. Both did, however, adopt a slightly different approach to working in the outdoor environment which may be related to the age of the children in their classes and the consequent expectations of other interested parties, such and parents and governors. For example, Leanne's activities tended to centre on features or natural materials found in the wild-life area. Molly, on the other hand, took with her to the woodland a variety of 'loose parts' from the classroom – materials (eg story books), tools (eg scissors, buckets) and practical resources (eg string, sheeting) – which the children could use to extend their play. Molly saw the outdoor environment primarily as a stimulating context to support children's play; to Leanne, it provided the stimulus for children's learning across the curriculum – although at least initially, she appeared to emphasise environmental education.

It has been argued that children have an innate sense of relatedness to nature and that effective environmental education can help to nurture children's sense of self as a part of the natural world (Phenice and Griffore, 2003). Some researchers (eg Wilson, 1999) maintain that if we want to ensure that children grow up caring for the natural environment, they need to have positive experiences of nature. Others argue that learning in the natural environment is not enough – even young children need also to learn about the environment and about how to care for it (Davis, 1998). While education about and for the environment was less noticeable in Molly's descriptions of her Forest School activities, it was apparent from her comments that her commitment to environmental education was woven through it and integral to her day-to-day activities.

Not only did both teachers modify the Forest School approach but they themselves were apparently changed by it! Both commented that their practice outdoors incorporated more child-initiated and child-led activities than their practice indoors. Leanne saw this as partially related to and a particular benefit of the Forest School approach. The shift in Molly's approach had been more gradual and appeared to derive from a growing realisation that the children were able to identify the affordances of the natural environment for themselves and to use them to develop their functional play – gross motor activities and skills such as running, jumping, swinging etc – construction play such as building dens, and fantasy play such as playing dinosaurs or cooking (see Fjortfoft, 2004). But Molly noted that children tended to divide up by gender in their play and repeatedly gravitated towards stereotypically male and female activities. This could be expected, since gender-typed behaviour tends to peak when children are around five years of age (Paley, 1984). However, practitioners may need to consider whether there is a case for intervening in children's gender-typed play: what are children learning from those experiences about the roles assigned to males and females? What experiences are certain children given access to while others are denied them? And how might this affect children's physical, cognitive and social development?

Conclusions

Molly and Leanne's initial understandings about Forest School resembled the Bridgwater College model: the primary focus is not so much on how effectively children learn particular knowledge, concepts or skills but the learning strategy itself and how far it supports the children's personal and social development. But Molly and Leanne were working in a statutory educational establishment, so had to meet, balance and integrate the needs and requirements of a range of interested individuals and agencies. In modifying what they perceived to be the Forest School approach they were making the best of what they had! It is perhaps unsurprising that the approach they eventually implemented moved towards the model of Forest School promoted by the FEI.

If Early Years' practitioners want to ensure that children develop as able, secure, confident individuals and as capable, motivated learners then, whether working inside or outside, considerations of what is learned and how it is learned are equally important. Katz (1999) notes research by Marcon (1995) asserting that curriculum and pedagogy should seek to optimise the *simultaneous* acquisition of knowledge (facts, concepts, ideas etc.), skills (physical, social, verbal etc.), desirable dispositions (eg curiosity, concentration, resilience) and feelings (eg competence, confidence and security). This was the position to which Molly and Leanne appeared gradually to be moving.

8

Movement learning: bringing movement into the classroom

Richard Bailey and Ian Pickup

Movement in the lives of children

Movement, sport and physical activity are significant in children's development and learning. Observe almost any child in almost any setting, and you will see ample evidence. Through playing games, young children learn about their bodies, their physical and social environments; they try out different roles and rules; they test their bodies and themselves. As they grow older, children learn how to become friends through playing games and discover how hard work and new skills can overcome obstacles. The benefits children derive from playing sports and games seem to be distinctive. As child psychologist Jerome Bruner observed: 'movement, action and play make up the culture of childhood' (Bruner, 1983).

Yet this is too often forgotten especially now that children are expected to deal with demands to succeed at school, be 'serious' and spend hours doing homework. Scandinavian writer Jan-Roar Bjorkvold (1989) suggests that there is a potential clash between 'child culture' and 'school culture'; between children's natural and spontaneous ways of learning and developing and their experiences at school. This is probably less the fault of teachers than the increasing demands on school time. Physical activity too often gets squeezed out of the timetable.

Reflect for a moment on the experiences of the children you know. Do their experiences reflect child culture? Are they playful, physical and

Child culture	School Culture
Play	Study
Being in	Reading about
Physical proximity	Physical distance
Testing one's own limits	Respecting boundaries set by others
The unexpected	The expected
Sensory	Intellectual
Physical movement	Physical inactivity
I move and I learn!	Sit still!

dynamic? Do the children approach the activities presented to them with joy and passion?

The most likely contexts for such joy are often provided by movement. Adults seeking to offer rewarding and enjoyable experiences to children should not forget this. Movement activities are among the most obvious and appealing ways of keeping in touch with child culture and bringing children delight and pleasure that may be missing from other parts of their lives. This alone is reason enough for such activities to be a central and regular feature of children's daily experience.

Children certainly seem to think that physical activity is important. Numerous studies have shown that the great majority of children enjoy a variety of forms of movement and recognise a host of benefits from playing. A recent survey of school children on four continents found that 86% either liked or loved physical activities in school (Bailey and Dismore, 2004). When asked how they thought physical activity helped them, most children agreed with each of these statements:

- it helps me be part of a group
- it helps me make new friends
- it makes me respect myself more
- it encourages me to go to school
- it helps me respect others more
- it helps me do well in school

Both boys and girls of primary age want most to succeed in sporting activities. Physical education lessons are among the most popular in school (Bailey, 1999).

Part of the appeal of movement activities is that they are socially prestigious. Sport and other physical activities are highly valued in our society, and children understandably wish to succeed at them. They watch their heroes in the media and aspire to be like them. We cannot tell how the phenomenon of the 2006 soccer World Cup or the 2012 London Olympics will affect children's views of sport, but experience suggests that both will stimulate a rush of interest among children to play prominent sports and to gather facts and figures about them. Children will probably be inspired to play sport at school and at home. Teachers need to recognise the power they have when providing movement – few learning activities have such appeal. Physical activity is that rarest of things: it is good for children *and* they love it!

In this chapter we suggest that teachers think again about the potential of movement activities in learning and see them not as breaks from the real business of education but as distinctive contexts for promoting the development of knowledge, skills and understanding.

Movement as a medium for learning

A class of children has enjoyed reading a story about a 'bear hunt.' The teacher asks the children how they could hunt for a bear or other animal in their school grounds. Some of the children comment that using eyes and ears to see and hear will be useful, and a child suggests that animals make footprints in the ground which could be followed. The class is divided into small groups, each accompanied by an adult, and they go outside to look for animals. Each group starts at a different place where the teacher has placed a picture of a footprint or track, along with a clue suggesting where the animal might be found. Each adult supports the children's work by talking about what type of animal would leave such a footprint, how it might move and where it might be hiding. The children move like the animal they are hunting; crawling, slithering, stomping with heavy steps or tripping lightly. Each group finds their animal – a soft toy – hidden around the school grounds and the children return to the classroom to describe their hunt to the rest of the class.

Virtually from birth, movement is part of daily experience. Gaining control over the muscles of the neck and back to remain unaided in an upright seated position, crawling along the floor, pulling up to standing and learning to walk are all ways in which children interact with their environment.

Early Years' practitioners start with the child and nowhere is this more pertinent than in the context of movement. Motor development is age-related but not age-dependent. The unique relationship between the biology of the individual child, the environment and the task in hand means that each child has different learning needs regarding movement. Child-centred movement activities are not just the preferred way; they are the *only* way. It is impossible to separate the body from the learning experience. The focus on the whole child in the early years allows us to capitalise on the 'thinking body' (Burkitt, 1999). Clark (1997) asserts that cognitive development cannot be treated in isolation from the child's physical self, supporting the long-held view that a healthy mind is linked to a healthy body (see, for example, Piaget, 1954).

Developments in multi-sensory learning have highlighted the importance of children's whole body actions when representing concepts (Athey, 1990), and Smith's (1998) approaches to learning raise practitioners' awareness of visual, auditory and kinaesthetic learning styles. Brain gym, recently introduced to schools, claims to strengthen neurological pathways, enhancing pupil attainment, concentration and behaviour through various body and mind actions (Dennison and Dennison, 1989; Hannaford, 1995). Whilst the scientific basis for such claims must be viewed with caution, links between cognitive and physical processes – the mind and body – are potentially beneficial. There is surely potential in utilising the body as a vehicle with which children can better understand words, ideas and concepts. Certainly it seems to be one way children learn effectively outside school.

There are countless ways children can use their bodies and their enthusiasm to be physically active to help them acquire basic skills and concepts in school settings (see Table 1 opposite).

Psychologist Ellen Langer's fascinating research suggests that simply being active can increase children's learning and retention of information. She argues that when children are inactive they often drift into a 'mindless' state in which they are not really attending to what is being taught. But encouraging them to move around their classroom as they engage in certain activities helps them become more 'mindful', and so more likely to learn and remember (Langer, 1997).

Whether considering teacher-led physical education activities, physical activity or play, a dual focus can be taken for learning. 'Learning to move' includes the learning of skills, techniques and understanding required for

Table 1: helping children learn through movement

Shapes	Holding hands in small groups, children recreate squares, circles and triangles
Spelling	Children make the shapes of letters using their bodies – first alone and then in pairs – to spell words
Numbers	As they run around a space – the hall or playground – children form groups of different sizes, according to the calls from an adult or child
Adverbs/Adjectives	Children suggest their own characters for new 'Mr Man' or 'Little Miss' stories, selecting words that describe movement and moving like the characters – for example: Mr Slow Mr Quick Miss Wobble Miss Bounce etc.
Modern foreign languages	Children travel around a space responding to verbal signals that are accompanied by written flash cards, such as (in French): stop – *arrêt* start – *début* run – *course* freeze – *gel* jump – *saut* tall – *grand* small – *petit*

taking part in various physical activities; 'moving to learn' uses physical activity as a context for learning, with potential outcomes across all developmental domains.

Many young children are restricted in physical play at home, so the Early Years' setting can give them opportunities to engage in physically vigorous activity. Young children appear to have a natural urge to move. Studies have shown that when children who are seldom allowed to exercise get a chance to do so, the intensity and the duration of activity increases (Pellegrini *et al*, 1995).

Movement provides young children with some of their first socialising experiences. Interaction with peers, adults and objects in the Early Years' setting is made possible through their fine and gross motor skills as children explore the environment. Movement helps young children to engage actively with experiences, to construct their own view of the world (Bruner and Haste, 1987), and to take an active, inventive role to reconstruct tasks through their own understanding (Smith, 1993). Interactive, active, collaborative, inventive and broadly 'constructivist' approaches to teaching and learning in the Early Years would be impossible if the children did not move about. By using a range of movements to work in collaboration with others, children begin to learn appropriate behaviours, share spaces and equipment, accept and respect individual differences, and solve problems collaboratively.

Children's learning in the physical domain, whether in play contexts or more structured teacher-initiated episodes, generally occurs in groups which require co-operative behaviours. Cognitive, social and affective development can be fostered through movement activities and this holistic approach is in keeping with principles of Early Years' teaching. Purposeful movement activities also develop bone and muscle strength, stamina and motor skill, and movement for health and lifestyle reasons is equally important. As well as being a holistic tool for learning, movement provides the key opportunity for physical learning.

Movement outdoors

Movement provides a vehicle for learning that can positively affect every domain of child development. Careful consideration is needed in order to create a multisensory learning environment for children. The outdoor context may be challenging to the teachers but it creates unique opportunities to bring learning to life in dynamic, enriching and stimulating ways.

> *In the garden, children have gathered around to look at hyacinth bulbs that have flowered during the weekend. They talk about how the bulbs were planted and watered and how changing weather has helped the bulbs grow into flowers. Observing the group, the teacher plans to use their interest and the descriptive language they use in a dance activity. Later that week the children are taken out into the garden, where they imagine that they are bulbs, planted in the soil. They make themselves as small as they can and then grow in response to percussion played by the teacher, imagining that they are pushing through the soil to the sun. The children bend, stretch and twist, concentrating on using different body parts at low, medium and high levels. Emerging from the soil, they respond in dance to the feel of the sun and the breeze as they grow and flower – the simple percussion guides and responds to their movements. The children develop their actions to represent other things that grow and share their ideas with their friends.*

Other chapters in this book show how the outdoor environment can provide a rich variety of learning contexts for young children. The nature of the environment is a strong predictor of physical activity amongst three and four year olds and they are more likely to be physically active outdoors than in (Baranowski *et al*, 1993). A large, well-designed space that makes use of surrounding natural environments not only enlarges the scope for movement but can provide varied stimuli for movement to draw on. Different textures, smells and landscape materials provide a rich context for physical activity and play and children appear to thrive on this (Titman, 1994).

The naturally occurring environment is probably the ideal context for play. Practitioners in settings which have trees, rocks and a variety of vegetation will see the natural lure of the outdoors to children It is almost as if a tree is saying 'climb me,' or a pebble next to a pond is saying 'throw me in'. If we want children to climb, what will they climb on? If we want them to slide, what will they slide down? If we want them to throw and catch, what objects should be to hand? The potential for variety and versatility of movement responses should be uppermost in the design of an outdoor movement classroom. Spaces to climb, balance, swing, slide, jump, land, run, skip, and hop need to be provided, along with opportunities for manipulative skills, such as throwing, catching, kicking, dribbling, aiming, controlling, and a chance to be still and calm.

Adults should consider their own approaches to scaffolding children's learning away from the classroom and seek to transfer teaching and learning strategies to the movement context. Giving children the chance to move will not by itself bring about learning; learning requires regular practice along with encouragement, feedback and instruction.

Movement across the curriculum

In the classroom, a group of children uses boxes, aluminium foil and coloured paper to build a spaceship. The children collaborate on the design and work together to complete the model. Some use scissors and glue to make instruments and accessories needed inside the ship, and others decorate the outside of the rocket. When the spaceship is finished, all the children crouch down inside it and pretend to blast off into space – counting down from ten together. In discussion with the teacher, the group decide that they would like to land on the moon (the playground) – to collect moon rocks. The children get out of the spaceship in the playground, pretend to move like astronauts and collect rocks (beanbags) from inside craters (hoops) on the surface of the moon. The next day, the children invite some of their classmates to join them and they take it in turns to be astronauts and aliens. The aliens try to stop the astronauts from taking the rocks – by playing tag.

The Curriculum Guidance for the Foundation Stage (DfEE/QCA, 2000) provides a framework which allows practitioners to be flexible. Under Physical Development there is guidance opportunities for movement experiences. But, more interestingly, there are numerous examples of activities where movement is central to the learning process in the five other areas of learning in the Early Years' curriculum. And there is guidance that places movement at the heart of the learning process:

> Young children are active learners who use all their senses to build concepts and ideas from experiences. For example, children listening to music may clap their hands, bounce up and down or sway to its rhythm; children looking at larger or smaller clothes may try them on; a child who is visually impaired may stroke and feel a guinea pig to find out what it looks like. (DfEE/QCA, 2000, p20)

In each area of learning, Early Learning Goals and associated stepping stones, the CGFS reveals rich movement possibilities. For example, in Personal, Social and Emotional Development, Ellie's enthusiasm at acquiring skills at sliding illustrates her positive approach to new experiences (p32); in Communication, Language and Literacy, Pip bounces up and down in time to her favourite nursery rhymes (p60); Mathematical development can be demonstrated by counting the number of jumps between logs (p74); Knowledge and Understanding of the World includes discovering the local environment and working out walking routes (p96); and in Creative Development, Alexander is shown using his art work as a stimulus for dance with a partner (p120).

So movement is not something that only happens in a specific space within particular planned-for lessons such as Physical Education. It permeates the whole curriculum and the learning experiences that extend beyond it.

The way in which children begin to understand specific concepts appears to be linked to bodily and kinaesthetic awareness. For example, an understanding of the mathematical concepts of space and shape appears to follow Piagetian theory whereby children construct mental representations through reflection on action (Gifford, 2005). The task of following a treasure map – an activity that will ultimately be orienteering – requires significant mental processing to update directions and locations whilst moving. Clements (2004) argues that young children's understanding of space and shape starts from the self as the point of reference and that an understanding of navigation comes through a growing ability over time to remember landmarks, connect sequences, represent the environment with objects and reconstruct environments from plans.

Language development

Children's vocabulary can be enriched through a focus on the language of movement. Specific skills such as walking, running, skipping, turning, twisting, curling, dribbling and catching can be performed in different ways by changing the time, weight, space and flow of the action and describing the changes using adverbs. Thus modifying their actions is exciting for children and encourages variety, versatility and creativity in planning and performing movement tasks. As movement and language repertoires expand, children will move more imaginatively and confidently and will be able to describe and analyse actions with greater clarity and expressiveness.

Towards movement learning

Movement is often associated with activities outside the classroom – and by extension outside the 'real' business of schooling. It takes place either in specially designated areas like the school hall, or outside. Games, dance and so on introduce children to activities that might be the foundation for a lifetime of enjoyment and learning. But they represent only a fraction of the potential educational value of movement.

We have suggested some ways to 'let movement in' to everyday practice in nursery settings and classrooms. But we have also emphasised how that movement plays a central role in children's development and learning. Movement characterises so much of children's interactions with their social and physical worlds that we need to question the assumption that learning takes place only in the head.

So what might teaching and learning look like if we really did bring movement back into the classroom? How might learning activities be organised? What might we expect children to achieve? Could we bring together child culture and school culture, through the medium of movement?

9

Collect the Whole Set

Gill Hope

Educational and non-educational play

Although many of the books aimed at Early Years' practitioners eulogise about play, not all forms of play are included. It becomes clear that the approved kind of play is so-called educational play, play that develops children's particular valued attitudes and capabilities. Play is seen as important because it develops social skills and creativity, provides meaningful contexts for early literacy and numeracy and lays foundations for scientific experimentation. Play is an appropriate way for young children to learn because it is in the nature of young children to play and to learn and to learn through play. Homes that provide educational play of this kind are 'good' homes.

Left at home, or in the coat pocket in the cloakroom, is the beloved Power Ranger or My Little Pony, through whom children project their emotional imagination. These, along with most TV, video, internet and computer game themed toys, are deemed unworthy to enter the classroom. They are tarnished with the brush of commercialism. They reach the parts that educationalists choose to ignore. Educational theorists have created an imaginary world of childhood that is radically challenged by

- the TV heroes and their pals
- the cartoon characters that appear unbidden on yoghurt pots, socks and duvet covers
- the interactive games that provide play scripts, often with props that can be bought separately, for children to build on in un-

familiar as well as familiar circumstances in the company of barely-known others as well as best mates.

This chapter is about the role of these unworthy challengers to good play experience, the anti-heroes of the toy-box, or: What every child has at home but doesn't get to play with at school or nursery. We need to consider why.

Play and exploration

There is confusion between *playing with* and *playing*. Adults as well as children need time to play with and explore new problems before they can solve them. Scientists, mathematicians, chefs, artists, engineers and designers all play with ideas and materials in the course of their normal working lives. This is the kind of playing that is encouraged in educational play. This is why, when you look in the index of the most books on early childhood play, the references to toys are sparse. Play is often taken to mean free exploration of ideas, space, skills and materials, framed within, among others, the following contexts:

- cognitive – pre-literacy or pre-mathematical activities
- spatial – such as jigsaws and construction kits
- physical – climbing frames, clay, water, sand
- artistic – paint, textiles, cutting out and sticking on
- fantasy – role play
- social – any of the above done with someone else

The innocence of childhood – an educationalist's fantasy

Rousseau and his *Emile* have a lot to answer for. This first textbook on childhood was born in the Romantic Movement when Wordsworth was striding across Cumbria and writing about clouds of daffodils. The poetic imagination – in contrast to the scientific rationalism of the Industrial Revolution – condemned the 'dark satanic mills' and looked for New Jerusalem to be built in England's green and pleasant land. Children were no longer seen as repositories of original sin, to be subjected to harsh discipline, but as innocent, gentle plants to be nurtured and brought to flowering in Kindergartens – literally child-gardens.

Pestalozzi, Froebel, Montesorri, Isaacs and all the heroes of the early days of the Early Childhood Education movement, stressed the goodness of young children; their curiosity, their enthusiasm for learning; their joy in discovery and mastery. All of which could be harnessed to educational purposes so much more successfully than the harshness of drill and chanting. This is all right and proper and no one would want it otherwise. But this view of early childhood ignores the unfortunate fact that children, like adults, are equally fascinated by blood, gore, crudity, sex and violence, and that they would like to include these in their play too. But it has to be done elsewhere than in Early Years' settings, where good playing is expected.

Play as children's work – preparing for adult roles

The Protestant work ethic, said to underpin western capitalism demands that time is not frittered away but that everyone should always be gainfully employed or else the devil will find work for idle hands to do. The Puritans were so strongly against adults playing, even on their days off, that they banned theatres, dancing and maypoles. Children's play, therefore, needed to be justified by theorists as children's work. But children, like adults, only want to work for part of the time. They also want to muck about, have fun with their mates, watch TV, go window shopping and spend their pocket money on a whole range of emotionally and socially satisfying plastic and electronic products that are not work. As well as wanting to emulate adults at work, children want to emulate adults at play. They, too, want time out to do their own thing.

The video game and the TV themed toys provide moments of shared cultural knowledge that are leisure, not work, focused. They also provide solitary play time so that Mum can do the ironing in peace – but toys have probably always had this function. Family emotional bonding is just as likely to be happening in the scream of frustration when Dad missed going onto the next level by two seconds or when everyone cuddles up on the settee to watch The Simpsons or Coronation Street as whilst adults are... what? Taking the kids on an educational visit? Giving them small sized kettles, ironing boards and work benches to play with?

Denial of popular culture

Adults in positions of educational child-care engage in rhetoric about bridging the gap between home and school, but this often means school values influencing home practices rather than home culture entering the classroom – unless it is traditional ethnic culture. This must be extremely confusing to small children who are barely aware that they have an ethnic culture, clutching their Power Ranger ('Leave it in the cloakroom, please, dear!') in one hand and their chapatti in the other ('My gran made this for us last night' – 'Ooh, really, let's have a look!').

An unforeseen effect of this is that children who do not have school-type toys at home will not play as freely or creatively in school as those who do, simply because the toys there are unfamiliar. They will need time to examine and explore the play potential of these new things and to learn from other children how to play with them. The play scripts learnt from Nintendo and TV shows and the play props that accompany them – action figures and other collectibles – usually guarantee some common ground when meeting new children on days out, in airport lounges, in holiday hotels and chalet parks but are irrelevant in these strange new circumstances. Unfortunately, in Early Years' settings, these ready-made roles are often seen as uncreative, whereas the highly ritualised script of the Home Corner, including its gender stereotyping, is allowed to continue unquestioned.

'Non-educational' toys in school

So what are the reasons for excluding all these non-educational toys from Early Years' settings? Is it that:

- they are often made of brittle plastic that will break with heavy use?
- they offer a view of the world that is at odds with educationalists' idealised view of childhood?
- they are overtly commercial, whereas the commercialism of educational toy suppliers are covert, buried beneath messages of child development?
- they represent the corrupting influences of TV and the mass media?
- they are for fun, whereas as educational toys are for learning? For learning what?

Is the underlying message that work/learning is to be separated from play/triviality, and that 'learning through play' is still 'work'? My Little Pony can come to school if it is only for playtime?

To assist my investigations, I visited local toy and games shops and quote excerpts from my conversations with their staff below. Three main issues emerged that suggest some ways forward:

- consumers making choices
- cultural change
- child development in a cultural context

Consumers making choices
Known brands vs. own brands

> Me: Is choice influenced by TV?

> Buyer: Yes, definitely. Power Rangers are back on. Then it's 'Mummy I want it.'

> Me: How well do things sell that don't have a TV branding? I mean, you've got some really nice toys over there, a wooden castle and hospital sets and so on. Do they sell?

> Sales Assistant: No, not at all. They won't sell. (*Points to a Barbie-style doll with no TV brand*) We won't sell that. Even if it was a pound. That's been there for months.

Launched in 1959, Barbie embodied the commercial dream. As well as being tall, thin and fashion-conscious, Barbie needed a whole range of accessories, which had to be bought separately. No make-do-and-mend, dressing in hand-me-downs or getting her hands dirty. Barbie-hood is closer to the fantasy world of the make-over than to the common sense realism of making the best of things. Observing the popularity of Barbie and Sindy, John and Elizabeth Newson (1979) comment that, unlike most dolls of the time, Barbie/Sindy were promoted by name: 'What is being sold is not a figure onto which the child can project a personality of his own idiosyncratic choosing but a ready-made package: the 'Sindy' or 'Barbie' persona' (p138).

Can such character toys be used in the classroom?
Yes. They are ready-made clients and users for Design and Technology projects.

Example: Bob the Builder
Product Range: TV programmes, video, books, toys, clothing and furnishings, lunchboxes etc.

Classroom use: Use as a stimulus for making models of trucks and other vehicles from recycled resources. This offers opportunities to explore and discover how axles and wheels work. Levers can be used for tip-up trucks and syringes and balloons connected with plastic tube for realistic control effects.

Example: Power Rangers

Product Range: TV programmes, video games, action figures including accessories which interlock to produce larger toys, dressing up clothes, play props – weapons, morphers etc – videos, books, toys, clothing and furnishings, lunchboxes etc.

Classroom use: A theme of the Power Rangers programmes is that at some stage the enemy will quadruple in size and will require the Power Rangers to combine their weapons or Zords to produce a Megazord which can defeat the enemy. Many children will already have examined ways in which these toys and others are designed to transform and this can be exploited in the classroom. Ask children to design toys which fit together to make a bigger toy, thus drawing on what they already know and teaching children a range of ways to join materials. There is an additional underlying message of co-operation – working together to defeat a common enemy – which can be discussed. Some practitioners may be uncomfortable with the violence in the show but children can benefit from discussion of such issues (see Marsh and Millard, 2000).

Example: Barbie

Product Range: TV programmes, video, films, books, toys, accessories – clothes, vehicles, furniture, pets, jewelry – clothing and furnishings, lunchboxes etc.

Classroom Use: A major frustration for Barbie doll enthusiasts is the fact that her limbs aren't jointed and can't easily be bent! So the vehicles designed for Barbie have to take this into account. An activity which examines a range of the vehicles and then asks children to design their own will provoke discussions about the design issues – including discussions about why Barbie's arms and legs aren't jointed in the first place. And her clothes can be examined – many of the shoes fall off or don't fit, her fixed splayed hands mean that clothes with sleeves are difficult to put on and take off; it is difficult for her to hold any of her bags or other accessories. Such discussions can get children thinking carefully about what will work best for Barbie dolls and why. Similar dolls can also be discussed and perhaps compared and criteria for judging what makes a doll 'good' could be considered.

Age Range: All these examples can be used across Foundation Stage and Key Stages One and Two, increasing the technical demand with age and having younger children as users of the toy to engage older children in the task.

Children's choices/parents choices

I asked my High Street toy shop informant what *children* buy. It was clear that children rarely went into the educational toy shop to spend their pocket money but preferred the general toyshop:

> Me: What is your most popular toy at the moment, what do children buy most?

> Buyer: There is no current craze line Football stickers, they buy.

The phrase 'craze line' appealed to me, as it implies children's choices, children's culture, beyond advertising and TV ratings. I learned about crazes that had taken them by surprise, when demand way outstripped supply and then the craze stopped without warning and they were left with Tamagotchis or whatever on the shelf that would never ever sell, because the moment had passed.

Despite anecdotal evidence from mothers:

> Lorraine: Power Rangers! Every two years they bring out a new set.

> Catherine: Yes – Bionic Rangers or something we're onto now.

> Lorraine: Yes and they have to have the latest ones, last year's won't do!

the demanding child, manipulated by media forces and advertising agencies to coerce money out of parental purses and bank accounts, did not seem to be a dark presence on my local High Street. For example:

> Me: What about bigger toys that they can't buy with their own money?

> Buyer: It's parent choice really, what they want them to have.

Looking around the pound-shops and bargain-stores, TV-related merchandise was rare. Yet these stores were full of children spending pocket money on cheap sweets and plastic trinkets, in contrast to the few customers in the large stores – allowing their staff time to talk to me – and where I saw no children shopping without parents. Perhaps children are cannier than most commentators suspect. Perhaps they are the buy-one-get-one-free generation, going for quantity rather than quality. They will only collect the whole set if it's on special offer, or if someone else is paying.

Learning to be consumers in the class shop

'As the child learns to shop, it also learns to be a particular sort of child.' (Kenway and Bullen, 2001, p35). As the child plays at shopping, that particular sort of shopper can be re-enforced or challenged within the play scenario. Children's most frequent experiences of shopping are the super-market or shopping mall and the swipe card machine. By contrast, the class shop is often the 'queue up to be served' kind rather than one with the products on shelves for children to pick up, examine, choose or put back. If the class shop is set up like a superstore, selling a wide range of goods, using recycled packaging from real products on the shelves to play at buying, then adults can role-play being customers alongside the chil-dren and discuss choices, costs, methods of payment and so on in a non-invasive and non-judgemental context. Appropriate environmental print could appear on realistic shop-style notices:

- Buy one-get one free!
- Special offer!
- Sale price!
- Reduced!
- Queue here
- No smoking

Literacy Links: Play with the genre of advertising slogans. Children will know all the jingles – can they create their own? Develop a sense of rhyme, alliteration, rhythm and fun in creating new slogans, captions and advert lines.

Cultural change
The myth of an ever-quickening pace of change

> Just as there are human genes with no instructions other than to resist mutation, there seem to be human beings with no other programming than to resist cultural change. (Rushkoff, 1996, p16)

There also seem to be human beings who believe that the pace of change is ever quickening and that society is headed for melt-down, but what struck me most of all in my toy shop visits for this chapter, was how little has changed in the last 25 years, including the prices, which had barely risen. Many of the toys on sale had peopled my son's toy boxes a quarter of a century ago: Masters of the Universe, Thomas the Tank Engine, Play-mobil and Lego. Apart from one new entrant, King Kong, all the TV-related toy ranges have been on the market since before I stopped teaching five year olds in 2002. Expecting to have to catch up with the current scene, I found myself instead walking amongst familiar faces. Power Rangers, who joined the club in the late 1990s, are still with us.

In *The Play Ethic* (2004) Pat Kane calls his generation (1970s children) the Lego generation. He recalls with obvious relish the emotional satisfaction of the feel and fit of the bricks and what could be made with them, his joy in visiting Legoland Windsor and seeing all the castles and dinosaurs made out of the little bricks. My son (now 27) recalls Lego with similar fondness and admitted that he and his friends had recently discussed their Lego. When these young men have children, they will be lying on the floor building Lego kits with the kids much as previous generations of Dads were ribbed about the train set.

This kind of continuity of play practice across generations is vital. Yet adults in schools and Early Years' settings seldom play with the children. They choose and set up what will be played with today and then take no further role in the activity. Fear of losing one's dignity, of it getting out of hand, of not being in control keeps the adult firmly in the teacher role. However, young children often have a limited repertoire of play themes or of techniques with construction kits like Lego and their play can be greatly enhanced when an adult joins in.

The new area of playthings is the video games market, yet one of the most remarkable comments I heard in my High Street toy shop visits was by a lady in the video games store talking about games for the youngest children: 'It depends whether Mum has time to spare to sit with them, really.'

How much has really changed? Parents who play games, play games with their children. Parents who don't play, don't. It rests with the playfulness of the adult, not the technology of the game. Millar (1968) concluded that the play of children reflects the playfulness of adults within their own society and that societies with a rich culture of music, dance, storytelling, feasting and festival had children who demonstrated a richer imaginative life in their play. All that has changed, it seems, is the technology.

Consumer education for kids

One of the inherent problems with moral education, healthy eating or consumer awareness is that the teacher can become seen as a kill-joy, somebody who doesn't understand, and, in the final analysis, a hypocrite. We are all swayed by advertising. We are all collectors and consumers. So let's be honest about it:

- Ask children to tell/write down what they collect – and you do the same.

- Ask how many collect particular kinds of toys. Tell them what you collect – ask if their Mums/Dads collect these items. Tell them about what your children/nephews and nieces collect.

- Discuss why we collect things.

Depending on the age and sophistication of the children, the kinds of issues raised in this chapter can be discussed:

- Does TV influence choice?

- What is the role of advertising/how does it work?

- Does what your friends have influence your choice of toys? Why?

Aim for honest discussion that does not patronise, that shows respect towards children's choices and desires, helps them to develop meta-cognitive skills and become aware of their own thinking and reasoning, as well as raising awareness of commercialism and marketing.

Older children could design a set of collectibles intended for younger children. This will enable them to appreciate the way manufacturers

- research their market and key into the desires and interests of target audience

- generate design ideas that can be adapted to a range of consumable products

- use characterisation and storyline to help consumers identify with the product

This could form a project that links Design and Technology, PSHE, citizenship, literacy and ICT, in which children could make their own animated advertisement, using drawings or moldable materials, and take digital photographs that can be imported into a simple animation package (eg Windows Movie Maker).

Child development in a cultural context

Educational Toy Shop

> Me: What about boys, then? What do they go for?

> Young Man: Seasonal stuff. At the moment it will be footballs.

General Toy Shop

> Me: What else is popular?

> Buyer: It depends on the weather really. Football, obviously, because of the World Cup. But you get some sunny days and they're all in here for their footballs and cricket sets.

The young man in the educational toy shop was unaware of the influence of popular culture on sales of particular products, and I saw almost no reference to popular culture in their range of toys.

Me: Most of your products seem to be own brand; why is that?

Young Man: We aim to sell toys that are educational but fun.

I found I was not surprised that their best selling lines were for ages 0-2 years, when parents want the best for their children and children are not yet aware of the wider social context in which they are growing up. Is such culture-blindness 'educational'? With the work of Vygotsky (1978) and social constructivism so deeply influencing educational thought, is a view of education as separate from the world of home, television and popular culture appropriate?

Play props and place-markers
Metaphor and analogy – the ability to make one thing stand for another – is a primary human characteristic that can be seen in children's play, is explicitly encouraged in educational settings and accepted without comment at home. For the educationalist, developing skills of analogical transfer and metaphorical understanding are essential for developing literacy and numeracy skills. At home, the virtual world of fantasy, whether involving physical or electronic props, keeps children happily occupied with little reference to the development of intellectual or cognitive skills. The targets of education, after all, are clearly defined. The aims of play are self-fulfilling. Yet there is overlap: children who play well learn best. There is something intangible and ill-defined within the richness of imaginative play that enables children to write more creatively, listen more attentively, make greater leaps of understanding in all school subjects. The fear is that too many toys that are themed to TV shows and advertisements stimulate greed and will set in motion a decline in childish imagination and, hence, school achievement.

Conclusion – is this fear justified?
This chapter has explored some of the underlying issues surrounding children's play and current trends in toy purchasing. Children are trying to learn about how their society functions and how to be a good member of that society. The role of educators is to provide them with the knowledge, skills and understanding that will enable them to become full and successful members of society, and this includes their role as consumers. To ignore or reject children's learning to be a child within a consumerist

world is, ultimately, to reject what children are becoming and aspiring to be. Whilst educators rightly regard themselves as gatekeepers of a 'better way' than rampant consumerism and market forces, denial by omission of the cultural artefacts by which children measure their own place in society may, unfortunately, make school learning seem alien or irrelevant to the real world of childhood.

10

Children and their parents in schools: a package deal

Rebecca Austin

Introduction

What contact do you have with the parents of the children you teach in an average working week? You might chat to one or two before or after school; you may have a couple of helping mums who come into the classroom; you may have an appointment to discuss a particular issue. What do you know about these and other parents? Would you recognise the parents of every child you teach if you met them out of school? Do you know anyone's first name? Do you know which parents work and where? Do you know who has a special hobby or skill? Do you know who is currently dealing with difficult personal circumstances? Should you? Does it matter?

When practitioners take on the education of a child within the school setting, they take on the whole child – and this includes their parents. Whilst much of what practitioners do will be child-focused, there is an acute need for parent-focus too. There is no doubt that parental involvement in with their children's education is beneficial. Research evidence and government policies testify to this and many schools promote their partnership with parents with genuine enthusiasm. But while there have been increases in parental involvement in the last few decades, it is all too easy for parents to be patronised and marginalised in their role as 'children's first and most enduring educators' (DfEE/QCA, 2000), with schools setting the agendas and dictating the practices.

By focusing on parents and their needs from their perspective rather than the school's, practitioners can find ways for mutually supportive relationships to develop. The issues are complex. Parents are not a homogenous group, even though they are often, like children, referred to as if they are. So policies and practices in Early Years' settings must ensure that parents are treated as individuals – just as their children should be. Not all parents will be easy to work with – but then neither are all children – and there are likely to be issues which relate specifically to groups of parents or to particular settings. But if parents' needs and rights are taken into account, practitioners will find ways to work alongside them to the ultimate benefit of their children.

Research evidence indicates overwhelmingly that parents who genuinely don't care about their children and their schooling are few and far between (Hornby, 2000; Coleman, 1998). Some parents may lack confidence in their ability to support their children, others may be fearful of the authority that schools and practitioners represent and others may have different cultural expectations of schools and schooling, but the vast majority want to be involved with their children's education. Traditionally, it is the schools and settings which decide how parents can best help their children and the home-school partnership tends to be led by the school – how many home-school agreements are written by, or even with, parents? This chapter discusses some simple ways of seeking parents' perspectives so that the partnership is genuinely two-way and parents, their views, needs and rights are 'let in'.

What parents want

Unless practitioners start with an understanding of what parents want from schools, efforts to build bridges between home and school are doomed to fail. Practitioners cannot take the view that they know best and coerce parents into a narrow role which may, with the best will in the world, be difficult for them to sustain and may well be counterproductive. Crozier and Reay see the role of parents as

> ...supporters of and advocates for their children and as having the knowledge and understanding to ensure the most effective and positive educational experience possible for their children. (2005, pxi)

Based on interviews with parents in settings across the world, Hornby (2000) lists what parents want from teachers. They want teachers to:

- consult them more and listen to their points of view

- ▓ be more open and approachable
- ▓ be willing to admit if they don't know something
- ▓ contact them if they suspect their child has a problem of any kind
- ▓ treat all children with respect
- ▓ make allowances for individual differences between children
- ▓ identify and attempt to remediate learning difficulties;
- ▓ discuss their children's progress at effective parent-teacher conferences
- ▓ correct class work and homework regularly
- ▓ give regular detailed reports on their children's progress
- ▓ be involved with parent-teacher associations
- ▓ use them more as a resource in the school (p16)

These points are all eminently reasonable and there are no surprises. Parents may not be suggesting that teachers don't do the things above, but only that they don't do them enough. Parents don't want to take over the running of schools (Coleman, 1998), but they want to have confidence in the teachers who play such a significant role in their children's lives and they want the crucial part that they, as parents, play to be acknowledged and developed. It is easy to make false assumptions about parents and their desire and ability to work with practitioners if they can't make their voices heard.

Relationships

I started this chapter by asking how well you knew the parents of the children in your setting. I believe that teaching is founded on relationships: the children I taught best were those I felt I really knew, and the parents with whom I have had the most effective working relationships are those I got to know personally as well as professionally. Negotiating the professional and personal boundaries of parent-teacher relationships is a significant aspect of the teacher's role. Teachers who prefer to keep a professional distance may alienate some parents and inhibit real cooperation. On the other hand, personal friendships may make it more difficult to handle sensitive issues with the parents concerned. Some parents don't want to blur the boundaries between home and school or share personal issues with practitioners (see Ribbens McCarthy, 2005). Others may feel intimidated and excluded because of their own experiences of education.

Whilst the exact nature of the relationships that parents and professionals share will vary, there must be a basis of mutual trust. Practitioners have to examine their attitudes and possible prejudices towards parents. Hornby (2000) suggests that teachers may unwittingly hold unhelpful attitudes towards parents – such as seeing them as the cause of the children's problems, or as adversaries who have different goals and priorities or who themselves need help so cannot help their child (p6,7). Teachers' attitudes should be characterised by genuineness, respect and empathy (Rogers, 1980 in Hornby, 2000). Difficulties with parents are often founded on lack of trust from one or other side. If parents believe that teachers trust them, that trust is far more likely to be reciprocated.

Communication

A colleague of mine once sent a child from her Reception class home with a slip of paper on which were written the words the child needed to practise for the class assembly about the seasons. The sentence read: 'In winter we wear lots of clothes to keep us warm'. The next day the child's mother came to see the teacher. She was deeply embarrassed. She apologised for having forgotten her son's vest the day before and said she had made sure that he was dressed warmly today. Although parent and practitioner easily resolved this miscommunication, it could have damaged a strong working relationship. My colleague was particularly distressed that the mother assumed she would communicate a personal issue in such a patronising and demeaning way. On another occasion a biscuit manufacturer was running a promotion which enabled schools to claim free school trips in return for collecting biscuit wrappers. After I had explained this to my Year One class, one child told her parent: 'Unless we eat biscuits we can't go on any trips'. Not quite the message I was aiming for.

Underpinning the relationships between practitioner and parent will be how well they can communicate. Practitioners must recognise that it is their responsibility to establish links between home and school (Coleman, 1998, p142). Constantly using children as messengers between the two parties can lead to miscommunication and misunderstanding especially with very young children. Information needs to be shared in both directions so that all parties know what they need do to foster children's happiness, well-being and development.

Parents need information about

  ▓ the school – prospectus, newsletter, day-to-day details

- the curriculum – what their child is learning about
- their child in school.

Teachers need:

- information about the child at home and the parents' views of their personality, strengths and interests
- relevant information about home which might affect the child in school, such as the death of a relative, a health issue concerning the child, a sibling or a parent. The strength of the practitioner-parent relationship, and the disposition of the parents concerned will affect the extent to which personal information is shared
- information about the child's special needs
- routine information such as reasons for absence from school

Is the information you share with parents what they want and need? And is it clearly understood? How easy is it for parents to share information with you? Frequent informal exchanges are far better than the occasional official letter on headed notepaper, written in an off-putting formal style. Chats on the playground before or after school are likely to be a far better foundation for lasting and effective communication than formal parent-teacher meetings. The accessibility of the practitioner, both physically and in their manner, will be essential to forming positive relationships which ensure that information is effectively communicated.

Parents appreciate written communication from school that is:

- friendly – avoid formality or weightiness. In some schools the children produce a regular newsletter. Desktop publishing packages make it easy to include drawings and photos
- readable – jargon free, in straightforward language, in the languages the parents require
- regular and up-to-date – parents know to look out for, say, a fortnightly newsletter and can rely on the information
- accessible – bits of paper shoved in reading bags don't always find their way to parents. Posters on parents' notice boards or the school website help busy parents access the information they need, when they need it. A simple summary of key dates, for instance, can be helpful for parents whose reading skills are poor
- timely – give the dates and times of the school play or in-service training days a month or more in advance so parents can arrange babysitting or time off work

- repeated – information goes missing and is forgotten, and not all parents keep their diaries up to date
- respectful – parents may need to be asked to co-operate with a particular school rule or expectation, but this can be approached from a stance of mutual co-operation, rather than 'telling parents what to do.

Since my children have made the transition to primary school, I have become more reliant on their teachers to initiate contact and on their interpretation of my children's achievements and difficulties in school. I have less opportunity to be involved on a day to day basis and must put my trust in the teacher – something I have found far more difficult to do than I ever understood when I was the teacher. I don't necessarily want to check up on them or make sure they are 'working hard' – but because they are such an important part of my life, I don't want to miss out on what they're up to.

Parents need to know when and how they can talk to teachers informally as well as formally and teachers should ensure that parents feel as informed as they want to be about their child's experience in school.

Sharing information about children

Practitioners and parents need information from each other in order to construct a complete picture of the child.

> Parents are experts on their own individual child and their family culture, and practitioners offer expertise in this stage of children's development and learning. By combining these, the best opportunities can be provided for each child. (Draper and Duffy, 2006, p154)

As soon as an issue arises in school, let the parents know – face-to-face, by telephone or via the contact book or other written format. Parents want to know. The communication should be made sensitively and sensibly. Children's achievements in school should also be shared promptly with parents. A note in the home-contact book or a quick word after school gives pleasure to both child and parent. Some schools send home certificates when children have done well or give the children stickers or other rewards. Children are thrilled when their parents are told about their achievements in school. And parents love to hear about their children's successes.

Information is typically exchanged in schools by:

- day to day and face to face contact
- home-school contact books
- parents' evenings (usually termly)
- reports (usually annually)

The effectiveness of these depends on parental involvement in establishing policies and practices, and reliable implementation by practitioners.

Face to face contact

Many parents are around every day, so can be spoken to whenever necessary, before or after school. Be visible and accessible to the parents, initiate conversations about everyday issues as well as about their children:

> Sarah keeps talking about her new bedroom – how is the decorating going?

> Rajesh was very excited about his new bike – how is he getting on with it?

> Has Steven finished his Lego model yet?

Showing that you care about things that are important in their children's lives develops your relationship with parents. You can speak to children in their parents' hearing, showing your interest in them and involvement:

> Hi Max, I like your new haircut!

> Good morning Jenna, did you have fun at the swimming pool?

> Welcome back Kanika, are you feeling better now?

I know of parents who panic when they see the teacher heading their way across the playground after school, because it is so unusual. But if personal contact is the norm parents are likely to be less anxious when you have to approach them about a difficult issue.

Home-school contact books

Home-school record books are useful for parents who cannot be in regular contact. But these too have potential difficulties and both parties should understand their purpose. Some schools use such books to inform parents about their children's experiences in school, particularly in the Early Years, whereas many schools only send a reading record book home daily and more general information isn't included. The home-school contact books that are used effectively:

113

- have a clear rationale which is understood by both practitioners and parents
- are used consistently by both parents and teachers and given high status and priority
- regularly provide parents with photos or anecdotal evidence about their children's experiences and achievements. Some practitioners write comments daily in every child's book
- inform teachers about children's achievements and experiences at home
- are kept confidential between parent and practitioners, allowing personal information to be shared when necessary
- are not used just for difficulties
- are used so that parents see their value and participate in the process as best they can – they can for example stick a photograph or postcard in the book, without feeling obliged to write a comment too
- are integral to information sharing, and are used to inform parents of events in schools, ideas for collaborating with children at home, illness and absence etc
- are used to celebrate children's achievements over the term or year

Parents' evenings

Research into parents' evenings at secondary schools suggests that they are '...fraught with jeopardy and risk of censure for all concerned' (Walker and MacLure, 2005, p109). As both a parent and primary school teacher, I agree. If the day-to-day strategies described are taken on board and ongoing relationships are open and honest, the stress of parents' evenings will be less for everyone and there should be no surprises for either party. Neither party should feel they have to wait until a set time once a term to raise a concern. But schools first need to find out what parents want and consider how practice might be adjusted accordingly. Consider:

- announcing at the beginning of the year that there will be chances to meet staff at different times throughout the year which parents can sign up to. Parents who do not respond can be contacted by the school
- ensuring that the time is seen as an opportunity for teachers to consult parents as well as vice versa

- offering a crèche service for parents during evening appointments
- offering regular drop in sessions which focus on specific issues
- offering consultations by telephone as well as face to face
- offering regular home visits

Reports

Teachers are required to report annually to parents in writing about their children's progress. Reports that are depersonalised and merely record work covered rather than children's engagement with learning all become rather similar. Most parents prefer reading personal comments about their children. Friends who are parents but not teachers tell me they find their children's reports boring. They don't always understand them – particularly the results of statutory testing – and can't see what they're for. Because they are legally required doesn't mean that reports have to be stale or dull. Strategies for making reports more relevant and interesting might include:

- asking parents what information they would like from school reports
- asking parents what they find difficult to understand and how this could be made simpler
- using a friendly format and avoiding overly formal writing styles and jargon
- including a section written by children about their perceptions of their learning, achievement and needs – very young children can describe their likes and dislikes in school
- including photos, pictures, and examples of children's work. When my son left pre-school he brought home a CD-Rom containing about fifty photos of his experiences plus a brief paragraph from the pre-school manager. His progress and development was obvious, and a joy to watch
- writing the report with parents as part of a parents' consultation evening using shared knowledge of children to celebrate achievements and set targets together
- producing a class report copied to all parents, which summarises the topics and areas of learning covered. Individual, personalised reports can be sent as well

115

■ reporting on different subject areas at different times during the year, such as reporting on children's creative development after an arts week. Collate and update these into the end of year report

Conclusion

...much more collaborative and creative partnerships between parents and practitioners grow and develop when, through reflection and evaluation, practitioners question their own practice and challenge their assumptions about working with parents. (Langston, 2006, p9-10)

This chapter indicates only some of the ways parents and practitioners can work together. Schools need to consider how they lean on support from home, whether it entails expecting parents to supply costumes for the Christmas play or to be educators at home. What opportunities are there for parents to spend time in the classroom? How are they helped to understand their child's learning and development? How are they supported in their parental role? How do you make use of the skills parents can offer as a resource to the school? For each school and setting there will be different priorities and needs – but each can do more to improve relationships with the parents with whom they work.

In the words of Miller, Devereux and Cable:

The form that partnerships take requires complex professional decisions to be made, including what is feasible, given the nature of a parent body, and what is most appropriate for children's needs. (2005, p48)

Parents are not an optional extra. It is easy to pay lip service to the role of parents in schools but what is needed are practices which are established and maintained by practitioners who are as committed to the needs of the parents as they are to the needs of the children in their care. When practitioners put parents first in their policies and practices the children's experiences in school are greatly enhanced.

11

The whole wide world: developing young children's intercultural understanding

Helen Taylor and Rebecca Austin

Introduction

Most of the chapters in this book show how familiar, local places are a good starting point for work with young children. But children know there is a world beyond their immediate environment and are fascinated by the concept of the whole wide world and the universe. Michael, aged six, showed his developing understanding of local and global matters (DfEE, 2000) when he addressed an envelope to the Queen like this:

The Queen
Buckingham Palace
London
England
The United Kingdom
Europe
The World
The Earth
The Solar System
The Milky Way
The Universe
Outer Space

He understood too, that the earth is part of something bigger still.

Children show their awareness of the enormity of the world in their play, their questions, their drawing and writing and even in their choice of superlatives – how many mums and dads rest secure in the knowledge that they are the best in the whole wide world? This knowledge about the world and its size comes from direct and indirect experiences such as:

- family holidays abroad
- their own experiences of living overseas
- television and films
- internet sites
- books, magazines and comics
- Chinese, Italian and Indian restaurants in the local community
- food from overseas such as Spanish melons, Danish bacon, New Zealand butter and French apples or tinned or packaged goods
- dishes from overseas eaten in the UK such as spaghetti bolognaise and vegetable curry and traditional dishes eaten at home or elsewhere
- postcards and stamps
- money from other countries – particularly the Euro
- ecological issues such as global warming and threats to natural environments
- world news events such as the tsunami of December 2004, the events of 9/11, war in Iraq, Afghanistan, Sudan, and sporting events such as the Olympic Games and the soccer World Cup
- tourists and the tourist industry, including *bureaux des change*
- people in their school and community who differ in family background and origin, including refugees, immigrants, asylum seekers and travellers

All these are good starting points for work relating to the global community, whether by stimulating discussion or inspiring a longer topic for study.

> *The role play area in a Reception class is converted into a tourist information centre. The children visit a local tourist information centre to gather information and materials; some draw on their experiences as tourists. Asked what visitors from other countries might need, the chil-*

dren suggest: guide books in other languages, maps, maps with pictures, books to help them learn English, postcards to send home, somewhere to change their money into sterling, directions to hotels. Some children design posters, booklets and leaflets for the centre, inventing words to represent other languages as well as using words from languages that are familiar. Older children visit the centre, taking the role of tourists who are not fluent in English. The children from the Reception class who serve them can communicate with and help their visitors in a courteous and understanding way.

Intercultural understanding

Figuratively speaking, the world is becoming smaller, thanks to ease of travel, advances in communication and the spread of global industries such as McDonald's, Coca Cola and Microsoft. Some argue that the shrinking world is a good thing, as it draws nations together and puts the need for intercultural understanding high on the world agenda. Others suggest that globalisation erodes national and cultural identities and devalues diversity. Either way, young children need to know that there are people in their local communities and all across the world who are similar to them in some respects and different in others, with whom they can build positive, productive relationships.

Intercultural understanding is an essential part of being a citizen. Children develop a greater understanding of their own lives in the context of exploring the lives of others. They learn to look at things from another perspective, giving them insight into other cultures and raising awareness of the similarities and difference between people, their daily lives, beliefs and values (DfES, 2005).

Increased globalisation means greater interdependence and also increased contact with people and cultures from around the world. Practitioners in schools and Early Years settings should aim to promote knowledge of the world, its peoples and cultures, to develop the skills of critical thinking and communication and the attitudes of being positive, tolerant and open-minded and the challenging of stereotypes (see DfEE, 2000; Risager, 2004; Oxfam, 2006). Intercultural learning aims to give children the skills and attitudes they need to function with confidence in different cultural environments (Fennes and Hapgood, 1997) and eventually interact effectively with people from various cultures (Guilherme, 2004). Learning for intercultural understanding enriches the curriculum and provides excitement, challenge and enjoyment.

> *A class of Year 2 children discuss what they feel are the most important things about themselves and their lives. They draw or write down their ideas on hexagons which they fit together to form their own patchwork quilt. The children look at one another's quilts and discuss similarities and differences – paying particular attention to the things they didn't previously know about their friends. The quilts are then joined together to form one large display representing the diversity within the class.*

It could be argued that the curriculum for young children is already packed and that it is hard to fit in intercultural learning and learning about global issues. Or that the issues are complex and difficult to understand so should be left until later in children's education. Yet many of the ideas can be taught alongside and build on other parts of the curriculum, particularly Personal, Social and Emotional Development. Moreover, practitioners will be building on children's own lives and experiences. It will take children a long time to develop their understanding so it is good to start them thinking about the issues early on. Attitudes of openness and curiosity are more easily encouraged at an early age. According to Byram and Doye (1999), it is older children who are more likely to see their own culture as the only normal one.

Learning new languages

One of the greatest barriers to intercultural understanding is language difference. Teaching children new languages can be successfully combined with teaching for intercultural understanding. Children are fascinated by languages. The sounds of languages intrigue them and they enjoy pronouncing different words much as they do exotic words in their first language, such as the names of various dinosaurs. Children extend their understanding of their first language through discussion of the similarities and differences with other languages in vocabulary and sentence structure, and the written script.

Research shows that children are especially receptive to learning new languages in the Early Years (Blondin *et al*, 1998). The White Paper of the European Commission (1995, cited by Johnstone, 2004) recommended that all children attending school should begin another language as early as possible, in primary education or before. But despite evidence from research and practice in other countries, the National Languages Strategy in England (DfES, 2002, 2005) has targeted Key Stage Two for introducing new languages. Younger children certainly can and do begin learning different languages in Early Years settings – and earlier – but the content and pedagogy should not be a watered down secondary syllabus (Cameron, 2001). Young children are usually lively, motivated, positive, willing to have a go and anxious to please, so respond well to learning a new language and their positive attitudes may endure for the future (Driscoll, 1999).

Which languages?

The languages will be chosen according to the children's own language repertoires and interests, their parents' involvement and practitioner expertise. For example, the practitioner may choose:

- Turkish, because three children in the class speak it fluently
- Spanish, to help a child in the class who is emigrating to Spain
- sign language because a deaf child has joined the class
- French, because the class teacher has French A-level
- Swahili, as a follow up to a visit from an African storyteller
- German, because the soccer World Cup is being played in Germany
- Welsh, using souvenirs a child in the class brought back from her holiday in Wales
- Japanese, because a group of children have been playing Pokemon and are curious about the way it is written down
- Finnish, in order to welcome a Finnish family who are joining the school
- Russian, as the class teacher is learning Russian at evening classes
- Gujarati, because the teaching assistant speaks it fluently

As well as extending home languages, introducing languages which are new to all children helps practitioners make links to the wider world. But they may need training so they can make language learning meaningful for the children (Blondin *et al*, 1998). The object is not to speak the language fluently; knowing a few words of several languages enhances understanding of the many different cultures that exist. The teaching of a new language should go hand in hand with teaching about the culture or cultures with which it is associated (DfES, 2005), thus providing a natural path towards intercultural understanding.

During the soccer World Cup, each Key Stage One class adopts a competing country. All the children learn to say 'hello', 'goodbye', 'yes' and 'no' in a language spoken in their chosen country. They locate their country on a world map and discuss its customs, dress and food. They meet people who have first-hand experience of the country, and ask them questions that will challenge the prevailing stereotypes and generalisations about certain people and places. Their findings are celebrated in a whole school assembly.

Resources

Maps

Maps are essential in helping children to find out about the world. Maps in different forms and to different scales, in different languages and with a variety of features to interest children and will stimulate discussion and help to answer their questions about the world. There might be:

- wall maps
- floor or table maps
- jigsaw maps
- children's and adult's atlases
- atlases in big book format
- pictorial maps with various themes such as flags of the world or animals around the world
- children's own maps of their neighbourhood
- globes – inflatable and fixed
- historical maps
- Google Earth (earth.google.com) is a useful website that interests even the youngest children

Books and stories

Books are another starting point for discussion. Both fiction and non-fiction texts give information and insight into how other people live and act. Literary texts from one culture can be read and enjoyed in translation by people from other cultures. There are beautiful children's books in dual text format and these evoke interest and comment. The texts for children need to be chosen to help children extend their intercultural understanding. Books can enhance sensitivity and respect for other people and help break down stereotypes and prejudices. But practitioners should be alert to and able to identify texts which confirm stereotypes. For children to understand whether the ideas in the story are typical or idiosyncratic and how literally they should be taken may require discussion, and will deepen not just intercultural understanding but knowledge about texts in general (Bredella, 2004).

As well as factual books written especially for children, holiday guide books and brochures can be useful. Children enjoy browsing through picture dictionaries and these are available in a wide range of languages.

Media sources
Television, video, DVDs, computers and the Internet are all useful resources. Children will discuss ideas they have picked up at home. Some may watch films and cartoons from other countries and are likely to know that DVDs and computer games are available in numerous languages. Programmes for younger children such as Teletubbies feature children from other countries. Cartoon character Dora the Explorer speaks both English and Spanish and children watching are encouraged to respond to her in Spanish. This programme shows aspects of Spanish culture such as food and traditional customs. Children will be familiar with programmes from America and can discuss vocabulary such as 'sneakers', 'recess', 'sidewalk'. The portrayal of American schools in children's television can be compared with schools in the UK. World issues raised through news broadcasts or programmes such as Blue Peter can be pursued through related Internet sites in schools. And as Alan Peacock shows in the next chapter, there are excellent programmes and websites for children about ecological issues.

The National Centre for Languages provides a useful resource bank of Internet and other ICT sources for teaching new languages and commercially available computer and video programmes use interactive approaches to help children learn a new language. These could be part of the range of resources on offer to children, rather than being used in an isolated teaching approach.

Email exchange with schools and settings in other countries, sending and receiving photos and video material, may be simple to arrange and can provide direct, first hand information about other countries and a meaningful context for learning a new language. Video conferencing with children from settings abroad is becoming more accessible and allows children to interact with peers in other countries, making music, singing songs, reciting rhymes or practising their counting skills together in their respective languages. Muslim parents may need to be asked whether they are happy for their children to hear and make music (see Harris, 2006).

Children take the technology available to them as the norm. They need to be given an understanding of the lives of children in other circumstances, such as those growing up in rural villages. But images of poverty that nourish stereotypical thinking are to be avoided.

Collections
On-going collections of artefacts from other countries can be developed in all settings. Children can add to them throughout the year as events at home or school arise, or items can be requested to form the subject of discussion about, for instance:

- labels
- ornaments
- clothing
- food packets
- coins
- postcards
- magazines
- brochures
- music
- stamps
- arts and crafts

A nursery begins collecting greetings in different languages. The children's photographs are taken and a digital recording is made of them speaking their greeting. The pictures and sounds are combined on the computer so that the children can hear the greeting by clicking on a picture of the child who gave it.

Daily activities and routines
Practitioners should feel confident to do little bursts of language learning with young children and quickly switch back to English for the next activity. Extended lessons may be inappropriate for young children but listening to a story or joining in with a song are good starters. Only a little vocabulary at a time should be introduced and there should be plenty of

consolidation, repetition and practice. With the focus on oracy, praise and instructions can be given in various languages so the children learn more than nouns and can see the purpose to their learning. They should be encouraged to look and listen carefully while the practitioner points to images, or mimes and gestures, so developing learning and concentration skills. The enthusiasm of the practitioner will influence the children's responses. Practitioners can develop activities within the routines of the school day, for example:

- greetings at the beginning of the day
- routines associated with the register
- brief role play activities eg on a theme of shopping
- using puppets which speak in the target language or ask simple questions such as 'What's your name?'

Projects

School-wide projects can enhance intercultural understanding and build on language learning activities. Special visitors who can teach children a little of their native culture and language – parents, staff from specialist language colleges, students from overseas – can be invited into settings to set the scene for the projects.

Schools and settings often:

- take one country as a theme for a day or a week and plan related cross-curricular activities
- celebrate a variety of different cultural festivals throughout the year
- hold sports days featuring sports and games from around the world
- plan art and craft or music weeks which focus on a particular culture
- devote a day to food from around the world and include food tasting and preparation

Children are enthusiastic about charity projects for other countries, particularly well-publicised causes like Children in Need or Blue Peter appeals. Some settings sponsor a child in another country and this gives the children a chance to learn something about the sponsored child's life and country and the languages they speak.

Conclusion

All these suggestions are designed for incorporation into the Early Years taught curriculum. All areas of the curriculum offer opportunities to embed the teaching of intercultural understanding holistically, whether learning about key historical figures from other countries or creating artwork inspired by various cultures. Intercultural understanding should imbue the whole curriculum so that children have a wide view of the world in which they live and learn.

Children bring to school what their own families and communities do, and their developing awareness of how ways of being and doing differ around the world. Simple activities in the everyday curriculum will help them to further their understanding. In teaching for intercultural under-standing, the teachers themselves will become more alert to stereotyped views and aware of how to challenge them. They will develop their own thinking to be more open-minded, reflective and critical (Bell *et al*, 1989). The result will be an 'outside' that enhances the children's views of the world.

12

Using without using up: involving teachers, children and communities in sustainable lifestyles

Alan Peacock

The ethos of sustainability is embedded in our school's work and life. We have attempted to 'live' sustainability rather than to simply talk about it. (Headteacher, Cassop Primary School, Co. Durham)

Children are never too young to learn about the world around them, or to learn that their environment is fragile. This chapter shows how education for sustainable development (ESD) can be made accessible to non-specialist teachers and their pupils, and suggests ways to become practically involved in living sustainably. As the headteacher quoted indicates, this is feasible and rewarding with young children; Cassop won an Ashden Award for sustainable energy in 2006.

The best way to start is by considering what ESD will mean for young children, so you can feel more confident about dealing with complex concepts such as ecology, bio-diversity and sustainability – the new facts of life in a way that children will find interesting and relevant.

In a book for primary teachers, I used the idea of eco-literacy rather than ESD, to show that we need to understand, or be literate about, our surroundings (Peacock, 2004). The Big Idea here is that our lives, our small planet and all our actions are interlinked through networks. This is true of animals and plants, as well as our communities, businesses, technologies, oceans, weather and global politics. We grow corn to feed cattle, sell the meat to Europe, and import just as much meat back: why? What would happen if all the bees that pollinate plants were killed off? These are questions children might ask: they are questions about the web of life. So here are some of the key words:

ECO –
From the Greek *OIKOS*, a house.

ECOLOGY
The relation of organisms to one another and to their physical environment

ECOSYSTEM
A unit of organisms and their habitat (eg a rainforest, a pond)

ECONOMY
From the Greek *OIKONOMOS*, a manager of a household, or steward

Hence the links:

ECOLOGY
How we relate to our
Environment

ECONOMY
How we manage
our environment

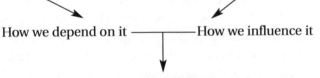

How we depend on it ———— How we influence it

ECO-LITERACY
Knowing about the consequences
of our actions (and inactions)

The world is inter-linked as never before: when you ring British Telecom, the call centre is likely to be in India. Children can e-mail each other almost anywhere. To live and work effectively, children have to learn how these networks behave, and how to use them to make their voices heard. They also have to think about 'what will happen if...' and to take responsibility for what they do.

Even in primary school, the boundaries between separate subjects are beginning to soften, so that learning can again be inter-linked and integrated. But preschool settings generally aim for a more holistic approach.

Learning about clean water supplies involves science, health, population growth, industry, culture, economics and politics. Two-thirds of the world's fresh water is in Antarctica: the icecap is melting rapidly. Whose responsibility is this?

The appeal to children of Eco-literacy

You may think that these issues are beyond the reach of young children – not so. In the 2001 *Guardian* competition to describe *The School I'd Like*, the idea of relevance figured strongly in the minds of children (Burke and Grosvenor, 2003). They want to learn about things that are in the forefront of their minds; and the future of the planet is one such issue. So perhaps this is a good time to consider incorporating the subjects children learn into something bigger, thus allowing its relevance to emerge more clearly.

Fritjof Capra, who coined the term Eco-literacy, is in no doubt about the importance of this.

> In the coming decades, the survival of humanity will depend on our eco-logical literacy – our ability to understand the basic principles of ecology and to live accordingly. Thus, ecological literacy, or 'eco-literacy', must become a critical skill for politicians, business leaders and professionals in all spheres, and should be the most important part of education at all levels – from primary and secondary schools to colleges, universities and the continuing education and training of professionals. (Capra, 2002, p201)

Eco-literacy can start, like the curriculum for the Foundation Years, by developing children's awareness of the world around them: materials, living things, weather, food, transport, energy. Small ideas lead to questions about big ideas: for example, how much greenhouse gas does your car put into the air during your trip to school? (A 5 mile round trip in a typical car produces 1kg of CO_2). From asking these small questions children will naturally move on to asking about the Big Ideas: the main principles that ecosystems have evolved to sustain the web of life – principles such as:

- networks: food webs, public transport, communities etc
- cycles in nature: water, carbon, nitrogen, the seasons, the gulf stream
- sources of renewable energy — by photosynthesis, solar cells, wind and water power

- biodiversity: protecting threatened species
- consumption and waste: recycling, composting, reducing landfill
- balance in nature

Children don't separate these ideas from other important things such as shopping, eating, clothes, music, TV, mobile phones, pets, sport. And in all these matters, there are decisions for them to make, which affect them and their environment. Which foods are really unhealthy ... is Jamie Oliver right? Where does this apple or this T-shirt come from? Is using a mobile dangerous? How do we prevent dolphins getting killed in fishing nets? Should animals be used for laboratory experiments? In other words, children often want to know if they are doing the right thing.

Children are also deeply concerned about the causes and unfairness of conflict, poverty, hunger, disease and who decides – ie politics. Many young primary school children were violently opposed to the wars in the Middle East, and came out to protest against it. Studying wars, trade, logging, mining, whaling, chocolate manufacture, oil drilling and many other industrial processes acknowledges children's fascination with studying other cultures. It also means that children see the way history, geography, religion and economics influence decisions. Issues such as these are issues because they provoke powerfully different views, things to argue about. They are big issues because they affect everybody on the planet, even though often we don't realise it. To take one example:

> Coffee is the most traded crop in the world, after oil. It goes through 16 stages between coffee bush and cup. At each stage someone makes a profit. The price of a kilo of instant coffee is about 7,000 times the price a grower gets for his beans. Is this fair? Who do you think is making most of the profit?

When children become hooked on this kind of learning about things that matter – even though they probably don't drink much coffee – they can do what they already love to do, that is re-design their living environment. But the choices are not easy: if cocoa bean producers were paid a fair price, a chocolate bar might cost a few pounds. Would they pay that much?

Eco-literacy therefore leads to thinking about such things as food production and distribution, energy generation, house design, transportation, in terms of sustainability i.e. using resources without using them up. The big question for children, as for ourselves, is always, 'Can you satisfy *your* needs without jeopardising the chances of *future* generations?'

Calculating the 'food miles' travelled by imported fruits, for instance, can lead children to think about how consumption of fossil fuels in transporting food could be minimised. It could also encourage them to start growing their own: children in schools in Amsterdam, for instance, are all entitled to their own school garden, a personal strip of community allotment on which they learn to plant and grow crops for themselves, and many schools in England are involved in the National Trust Guardianship scheme, which enables children to do regular gardening or conservation work in real contexts outside school. There are examples in this book of gardens in nursery settings too.

A local approach

This means that eco-literacy for children should have a local dimension. Sensible, 'sustainable' food production or water conservation would focus on different things in East Anglia, Cornwall or the Lake District, never mind in Mali or Zimbabwe. Children at primary level can debate problems like this:

> In a rural area of an African country, a British charity built a water pipeline to a village that had never had running water, and set up a tap in the centre of the village. Within days, however, the pipeline had been smashed in several places. Why? The nearest fresh water was a river about 30 minutes walk away: local boys had a donkey cart fitted with a large oil-drum, in which they collected water and sold it to villagers. The pipeline had destroyed their source of income, so they smashed it. What should be done?

Waste is another local matter. Recycling and waste management mean one thing to children in an agricultural area, something else in an industrial city. Sixty years ago, the contents of a domestic dustbin would have been 60 percent ash from coal fires. Now, your wheelie-bin is more likely to contain 60 percent plastic. The first question for children is not what to do about it – first they need to find out what the situation is in their area. Can we recycle plastic? If not, why not? Why do they have recycling bins in the nearby town but not in our village? How much would it cost to have weekly collections instead of fortnightly? These simple facts are suddenly seen to be connected to many other issues, such as the wage bill for refuse collection, EU targets for recycling and the demand for plastic – for instance, expensive fleeces are made from recycled plastic milk bottles in China. Schools across Somerset have benefited from a Waste Action Programme for several years, which involves visiting a landfill and recycling site, and having experts regularly visit their school to encourage recycling, composting etc (Vrdlovcova, 2005). The impact young children have made, not only on their school but on their parents' habits, has been extra-ordinary.

As the headteacher at Cassop school observed,

> Pupils at the school have become the driving force for change, promoting sustainable energy use in their community, acting as Energy Monitors in the classroom and Eco-Ambassadors, demonstrating their impressive knowledge and approach to local and overseas visitors.

Cassop has drastically cut carbon emissions by using renewable energy – a wind turbine, solar panels, biomass boiler using local waste wood – and energy efficiency measures. They display the school's energy consumption electronically, using a solar-powered device, and this shows impressive reductions. They host visits from other schools, are linked to a school in rural Kenya where climate change is already having an impact, and have supported the installation of a Photo-voltaic lighting system there. They also work with five European schools through the Comenius project.

And they are not alone. Buntingsdale Infant School in Shropshire has installed a Ground Source Heat Pump which uses energy from the ground to heat the school, saving them 18 tonnes of CO_2 emissions a year, or 70 percent of their energy consumption. Eastchurch C of E Primary School on the Isle of Sheppey has E-Teams, Energy Monitors and an Eco-code devised by pupils – 'We Use Energy Wisely'- which have become a key part of the school's ethos of cutting waste and energy use. Solar panels have been installed, low energy lighting is used throughout the school, and teachers run ongoing competitions on energy-saving tips. There are regular Community Action Days to involve parents and the local com-munity. In the kitchen, food is sourced locally where possible, to reduce air miles.

So clearly eco-literacy need not be serious, problem-ridden and joyless. The Schools' Art Projects at the Eden Project have been a powerful demonstration of how children can see the interdependence of plants, people and the global environment and celebrate it by creating paintings, sculptures, collages and fabrics. All over the world, music, drama, story-telling and dance are key ways in which people communicate important ecological messages about crops, rain, soil, forests, animals and their spiritual beliefs: the carvings and paintings of the First Peoples of North America and the music and dance of Africa and India demonstrate this powerfully. Closer to home, I recently watched young Cornish children creating a dance to tell the story of what they learned after a visit to an environmental centre. They were utterly engrossed.

Children can act in many ways: a 'you can...!' philosophy is the cornerstone of good eco-literacy. Many schools and preschools now have composting bins and worm bins, and children love exploring these, by smell alone. They take complete control of paper and card recycling. Primary schools can and do apply ecological principles: an Eco-schools movement is thriving and could be extended to nursery settings too. But much more could be done if schools and settings made links with each other. Focusing on eco-literacy will make partnerships more necessary – and more possible. Every school and setting is close to something like a landfill site, recycling centre, abattoir, supermarket, factory, farm, airport, harbour, nature reserve, building site, sewage works, power station or environmental centre. These are real places, where the real things that fascinate children go on. Direct involvement between children and such real-world sources of sustainable – or non-sustainable – activity are a valuable way for them to gain first-hand insights and add relevance and depth to their understanding.

What all the programmes have achieved – and there are many more examples – is not only heightened awareness of the need for eco-literacy, but also higher self-esteem amongst children, which adults see as arising from the participatory ethos and shared vision. It is not difficult. With a focus on eco-literacy, in both school and community, it is easier than you think to engage even very young children in sustainable practices.

Eco-literacy is about understanding how the many networks operate – how pulling strings in one place affects things in other, perhaps distant, parts of the net. The water network, for example, involves consumers (us), water companies (big business), farmers, environmentalists, industries that use water, people who live close to water, government, tourists and all the animals and plants that live in water and depend on it. An outbreak of pollution in one place can have an impact on many others. Under-funding of water treatment will also affect us all. Over-extraction of water in one place means a shortage somewhere else. Polluting the atmosphere with too much carbon dioxide could ultimately mean floods, rising sea-levels, the disappearance of much of Bangladesh. Tell the children the story about Easter Island (see below) so they can talk about and think through the connections in the web of life, and find out reliable information on which to base their ideas.

Easter Island: a parable for the world

The story of Easter Island raises many of the questions about ecology and survival that we face in the world today and is easy for children to understand and discuss.

Easter Island, known to inhabitants as Rapa Nui, is the most isolated island on the planet, being about 1,000 miles from South America to the east and Polynesia to the west, in the centre of the Pacific Ocean. It was first settled by Polynesians who arrived there in the 6th century, making the entire journey by canoe. They found an island rich in palm trees, birds and fish, and settled there. Slowly their population grew for about 1,000 years – then suddenly they disappeared almost entirely. Archaeological evidence shows that in the 16th century, many died of starvation; the island was denuded of palms; and most skeletons showed that the people had suffered violent deaths. What happened?

Sadly, this was not caused by an earthquake, hurricane or any other natural disaster. It was brought on by the islanders themselves.

Easter Island is famous for its many huge carved stone heads, some over 10m tall, weighing hundreds of tons, and they were the reason why life on the island ended. The inhabitants carved the statues as tributes to their ancestors; the stone heads watched over them and protected them. However, moving them into place was a huge task, and required many rollers, which they made with the palm trees.

Gradually, all the palm trees were cut down to transport more and more statues, and could not regenerate fast enough. So fewer and fewer birds nesting on the island survived. But the people there depended on birds and their eggs for food. And without trees they could not make canoes, so they could only fish from the shore. Food became scarce, people starved, and civil war broke out over what food was left. Many people were slaughtered. But without canoes, they could not escape to find other land; they were cut off by a thousand miles of sea. The population was reduced to a very few, who gradually learned their lessons and established systems for sharing the few remaining birds and their eggs, and growing a few crops to eat.

Then in the 18th century, Dutch explorers arrived. They found a small, settled, peaceful population that was beginning to recover. However, the Dutch brought with them the worst gift of all: diseases which wiped out the few people left, who had had no contact with European diseases and could not recover from them. Only the giant stones remain to remind us of this amazing culture.

Children can find out more about the story of Rapa Nui by searching the web for 'Easter Island'. One good site is the BBC's Horizon programme, on www.bbc.co.uk/science/horizon/2003/easterisland.shtml

Partnership means working together to prevent the kinds of disasters touched on above. Gaining publicity is often a key element in this, and children are excellent publicists of environmental problems. They care about fairness, and can be passionate about the ethical issues involved. If listened to, they will often go on to be active in environmental organisations or in their local communities, affecting local political networks in ways that their elders cannot. What we cannot do is ignore them, patronise them, imagine they don't understand or laugh at the points they make. Nursery is not too early to bring the world and ESD into the classroom.

The last word is with Michael Roth, a Canadian environmental educator:

> Rather than preparing students for life in a technological world, I work with teachers to create opportunities for participating in this world and for learning science in the process of contributing to everyday life of the community... early participation in community-relevant practices provides for continuous participation and a greater relevance of schooling to the everyday life of its main constituents. (Roth, 2003)

So take your pupils out into the real world to address the real problems that demand eco-literacy, and let the real world in to your setting or school so they can tackle issues there too.

Notes on contributors

Rebecca Austin joined Canterbury Christ Church University as a senior lecturer in primary education after more than a decade teaching in Kent schools. She works with student teachers and teachers to promote an understanding of the need to make learning in school meaningful and relevant to children. Her particular areas of interest are Early Years education and learning and teaching English in primary schools.

Richard Bailey, Professor of Pedagogy at Roehampton University, is a leading international authority on physical education and children's physical development. He has written the standard textbook for trainee teachers of physical education, and has worked for the International Olympic Committee, UNESCO and numerous government and charitable agencies.

Jonathan Barnes is senior lecturer in Primary Education at Canterbury Christ Church University. He has wide experience in further, secondary and primary education both in England and in the developing world. His international work has resulted in a strong inter-cultural and global character to his teaching materials. He has written a wide range of books and articles for teachers. His research interests are in promoting cross curricular and creative thinking in the primary school.

Gina Donaldson was a primary school teacher for eleven years before moving into Higher Education. She is particularly interested in children's mathematical problem solving strategies and the teaching of mathematical thinking.

Sue Hammond is a Senior Lecturer in Primary Education, teaching both English and Early Years education. She is involved in research projects related to literacy development working with children and teachers. Sue draws on more than 20 years' teaching experience in order to promote a holistic approach to learning in the Early Years both in and out of the classroom.

Dr. Gill Hope is a senior lecturer in Primary Design and Technology at Canterbury Christ Church University. Prior to this she taught on the Isle of Sheppey, Kent for 15 years, where she also conducted the research for her Ph.D in young children's use of drawing to develop design ideas. She is a member of the Design and Technology Association (DATA) Advisory Board for Initial Teacher Education and a regular contributor to conferences and journals.

Dr Trisha Maynard is currently the Head of the Department of Childhood Studies at Swansea University. Trisha's research interests include early childhood education, young children and gender as well as outdoor play and learning.

Dr Alan Peacock is a former teacher educator and Reader in Primary Science at the University of Exeter. He is the author of a number of books including *ECO-Literacy for Primary Schools*.

Ian Pickup is currently Principal Lecturer in Physical Education at Roehampton University, leading the distinctive primary PE specialist pathway to QTS. Previous roles have been teacher, sports development officer and professional rugby player.

Ian Shirley is a senior lecturer in primary music education at Canterbury Christ Church University. He worked for many years in primary schools and now leads a project entitled 'Strangely Familiar' that seeks to help student teachers rediscover the excitement and curiosity of childhood and learning, particularly through cross curricular and self-initiated activity.

Helen Taylor is a Senior Lecturer in Primary Education at Canterbury Christ Church University. Her interest in mainly in Primary Mathematics but she is also involved in the management of Primary Modern Foreign Languages.

Terry Whyte is a Senior Lecturer in Education at Canterbury Christ Church University specialising in Geography. His particular interest is in developing the use of the local environment to help young children to develop a sense of citizenship, belonging and wonder.

Jane Williams-Siegfredsen is lecturer in pedagogy at University College Jutland and an independent consultant and trainer for *Inside-Out Nature*, specialising in courses in the UK and Denmark about how to develop pedagogical practices in learning environments. She has given conference presentations and written about how children develop their skills and competences in the outdoors.

References

Alexander, R. (2000) *Culture and Pedagogy* Oxford: Blackwell

Anning, A., Cullen, J. and Fleer, M. (2004) *Early Childhood Education* London: Sage

Arts Council (1990) *The Arts 5-16* London: Oliver and Boyd

Athey, C. (ed) (1990) *Extending Thought in Young Children: A parent-teacher partnership* London: Paul Chapman Publishing

Atkinson, S. (1992) *Mathematics with Reason* Oxon: Hodder and Stoughton

Ashton, E. (2000) *Religious Education in the Early Years* London: Routledge

Bailey, R.P. (1999) Physical Education, Action, Movement and Play, in Riley, J. and Prentice, R. (eds) *The Primary Curriculum 7 – 11* London: Paul Chapman Publishing

Bailey, R.P. and Dismore, H. (2004) Sport in Education: the role of physical education and sport in education Project Report to 4th International Conference of Ministers and Senior Officials Responsible for Physical Education and Sport (*MINEPS IV*) Berlin: International Council for Sport Science and Physical Education

Ball, S.J. (2004) (ed) *The RoutledgeFalmer Reader in Sociology of Education* London: RoutledgeFalmer

Baranowski, T., Thompson, W.O., DuRant, R.H., Baranowski, J. and Puhl, J. (1993) Observations on Physical Activity in Physical Locations: Age, Gender, Ethnicity, and Month Effects *Research Quarterly for Exercise and Sport* 64(2) pp127-133

Barnes, J. and Shirley, I. (2005) Strangely Familiar *British Education Research Association Annual Conference* University of Glamorgan 14-17 September

Bell, G. H., Miles, A. G. and Ovens, P. (eds) (1989) *Europe in the Primary School: In England, A Case Study* Sheffield: PAVIC Publications

Bilton, H. (2002) *Outdoor Play in the Early Years: Management and Innovation* (2nd Edition) London: David Fulton

Bishop, J. and Curtis, M. (2003) *Play Today in the Primary School Playground: Life, Learning and Creativity* Buckingham: Open University Press

Bjorkvold, J-R. (1989) *The Muse Within – Creativity and Communication, Song and Play from Childhood through to Maturity* New York: HarperCollins

Blondin, C., Candelier M., Edelenbos, P., Johnstone, R., Kubanek-German, A. and Taeschner, T. (1998) *Foreign Languages in Primary and Pre-School Education: A Review of Recent Research within the European Union* London: CILT

Bowles, R. (1998) Defining Localities, in Scoffham, S. (ed) *Primary Sources: research findings in Primary Geography* Sheffield: Geographical Association

Bredella, L (2004) Literary texts and Intercultural Understanding, in Byram M. *Routledge Encyclopedia of Language Teaching and Learning* London: Routledge

Brice-Heath, S. and Wolf, S. (2004) *Art is all about Looking: Drawing and Detail* London: Creative Partnerships

Bridgwater College Forest School Available at: http://www.bridgwater.ac.uk/sites/forestschool (Accessed: 2 June 2006)

Bruce, T. (2005a) *Developing Learning in Early Childhood* London: Paul Chapman Publishing

Bruce, T. (2005b) *Early Childhood Education* London: Hodder Arnold

Bruner, J. (1983) *Child's Talk – Learning to Use Language* Oxford: Oxford University Press

Bruner J. and Haste, H. (eds) (1987) *Making Sense: the child's construction of the world* New York: Methuen

Burke, C. and Grosvenor, I. (2003) *The School I'd Like: Children and young people's reflections on an education for the 21st century* London: RoutledgeFalmer

Burkitt, I. (1999) *Bodies of Thought: Social Relations, Activity and Embodiment* London: Sage

Byram, M and Doye, P (1999) Intercultural Competence and Foreign Language Learning in the Primary School, in Driscoll, P. and Frost, D. *The Teaching of Modern Foreign Languages in the Primary School* London: Routledge

Cameron, L. (2001) *Teaching Languages to Young Learners* Cambridge: CUP

Cameron, C. (2005) Independence and Risk in Early Childhood Settings: Providing Opportunities for Discussion, *Early Childhood Folio 9* New Zealand Council for Educational Research.

Capra, F. (2002) *The Hidden Connections: A science for sustainable living* London: Harper Collins

Carr, W. (2005) (ed) *The RoutledgeFalmer Reader in Philosophy of Education* London: RoutledgeFalmer

Clark, A. (1997) *Being There: Putting Brain, Body and World Together Again* London: MIT Press

Clark, M.M. (2005) *Understanding Early Childhood Education: the Relevance for the future of lessons from the past* Abingdon: RoutledgeFalmer

Claxton, G. (1997) *Hare Brain Tortoise Mind* London: Fourth Estate

Clements, D. H. (2004) Perspective on the child's thought and geometry, in Carpenter, T.P., Dossey, J.A. and Koehler, J.L. (eds) *Classics in mathematics education research* Reston, VA: National Council of Teachers of Mathematics.

Coleman, P. (1998) *Parent, Student and Teacher Collaboration – the Power of Three* London: Paul Chapman Publishing

Copenhagen Council (2003) *Forældres og personales syn på dagtilbuddene I Københavns kommune januar* (Parents' and personnel's vision of childcare provision in Copenhagen's local council)

Costello, P. (2000) *Thinking Skills and Early Childhood Education* London: David Fulton

Crozier, G. and Reay, D. (2005) *Activating Participation – Parents and Teachers Working Towards Partnership* Stoke on Trent: Trentham

Csikszentmihalyi, M. and Csikszentmihalyi, S. (eds) (1992) *Optimal Experience: Psychological Studies of Flow in Consciousness* Cambridge University Press

David, T., Goouch, K. and Powell, S. (2005) Research Matters, in Abbott, L. and Langston, A. (eds) *Birth To Three Matters* Buckingham: Open University Press

Davis, J. (1998) Young Children, Environmental Education and the Future *Early Childhood Education Journal* 26 (2) pp117-123

Dennison, P. and Dennison, G. (1989) *Brain Gym: Teacher's Edition* Ventura, CA: Edu-Kinaesthetics

Dewey, J. (1929) My Pedagogic Creed, in Flinders, D.J. and Thornton S.J. (1997) (eds) *The Curriculum Studies Reader* London: Routledge

DfEE (2000) *Developing the Global Dimension in the School Curriculum* DFID/DfEE/QCA/Development Education Association/The Central Bureau

DfEE/QCA (2000) *Curriculum Guidance for the Foundation Stage* London: QCA

DfEE/QCA (1999) *The National Curriculum: Handbook for Primary Teachers in England Key Stages 1 and 2* London: DfEE/QCA

DfES (2002) *Languages for All: Languages for Life. A Strategy for England* Nottingham: DfES

DfES (2004) *Every Child Matters: Next Steps* Nottingham: DfES

DfES (2005) *The Key Stage 2 Framework for Languages* Nottingham: DfES

Donaldson, M. (1978) *Children's Minds* London: Croom Helm

Draper, L. and Duffy, B. (2006) Working with Parents, in Pugh, G. and Duffy B. (eds) *Contemporary Issues in the Early Years* (4th Edition) London: Sage

Driscoll, P. and Frost, D. (eds) (1999) *The Teaching of Modern Foreign Languages in the Primary School* London: Routledge

Dunne, J. (1995) What's the Good of Education?, in Wilfred Carr (ed) (2005) *The RoutledgeFalmer Reader in Philosophy of Education* London: RoutledgeFalmer

Edwards, R. (2002) (ed) *Children, Home and School: Regulation, Autonomy or Connection?* London: RoutledgeFalmer

Factor, J. (2004) Tree Stumps, Manhole Covers and Rubbish Tins: The Invisible Playlines of a Primary School Playground *Childhood* 11(2) pp142-154 Sage Publications [Online]. Available at: http://chd.sagepub.com/cgi/content/abstract/11/2/142 (Accessed: 19 August 2006)

Fennes, H. and Hapgood, K. (1997) *Intercultural Learning in the Classroom; Crossing Borders* London: Cassell

Fjortoft, I. (2004) Landscape as Playscape: the effects of natural environments on children's play and motor development, *Children, Youth and Environments* 14 (2) pp21-44

Flinders, D.J. and Thornton, S.J. (1997) (eds) *The Curriculum Studies Reader* London: Routledge

Forest Education Initiative Available at: http://www.foresteducation.org/about_fei.php (Accessed: 2 June 2006)

Gardner, H. (1999a) *Intelligence Reframed, Multiple Intelligences for the 21st Century* New York: Basic Books

Gardner, H. (1999b) *The Disciplined Mind* New York: Simon and Schuster

The Geographical Association (2003) *Making Connections: Geography in the Foundation Stage – a Position Statement from the Geographical Association* Sheffield: Geographical Association

Gifford, S. (2005) *Teaching Mathematics 3-5: Developing Learning in the Foundation Stage* Buckingham: Open University Press

Google Earth (2006) Available at: http://earth.google.com (Accessed: 20 July 2006)

Goouch, K. (2005) Places and Spaces: the Right Environment for Literacy, in Lambirth, A. (ed) *Planning Creative Literacy Lessons* London: David Fulton

Gopnik, A., Meltzoff, A. and Kuhl, P. (1999) *How Babies Think* London: Weidenfield and Nicolson

Grahn, P., Mårtensson, F., Lindblad, B., Nilsson, P. and Ekman, A. (1997) *Ute på dagis* (Outside in the Day Nursery) Alnarp Sweden Forlag Movium

Grainger, T, Barnes, J. and Scoffham, S. (2006) *Creativity for Tomorrow. Research report*, Margate: Creative Partnerships.

Great Limber Forest School Available at: http://beehive.thisisscunthorpe.co.uk/default.asp?WCI=SiteHomeandID=7501andPageID=39973 (Accessed: 2 June 2006)

Groundwater-Smith, S. (2004) Transforming Learning: Transforming Places and Spaces for Learning *Design and Learning: Has the Paradigm Changed?* CEFPI Conference Facility Conservatorium of Music, Sydney 21 April 2004. Available at: http://australasia.cefpi.org/pdf/SusanGroundwaterSmith2004Paper.doc (Accessed: 29 August 2006)

Guilherme, M. (2004) Intercultural Competence, in Byram, M. *Routledge Encyclopedia of Language Teaching and Learning* London: Routledge

Hannaford, C. (1995) *Smart Moves. Why learning is not all in your head* Arlington, VI: Great Ocean Publishers

Hansen, M. (2003) Kolbøtter, kundskaber og magi (Somersaults, Knowledge and Magic), in Christiansen, J.L., Hyllested, T., Nielsen, S., Paulsen, A.B. and Petersen, B. (eds) *Børn og nature – hvorfor og hvordan?* (Children and Nature – Why and How?) Gylling Denmark: Narayana Press

Harris, D. (2006) *Music Education and Muslims* Stoke on Trent: Trentham Books

Hart, R. (1979) *Children's Experience of Place* New York: Irvington Press

Herholdt, L. (2003) *Sprogbrug og sprogfunktioner i to kontekster* (Language and its use in Two Contexts) Denmark, Danmarks Pædagogogiske Universitet Forlag

Hicks, D. (2002) *Lessons for the Future: the Missing Dimension in Education* London: RoutledgeFalmer

Hillman, M. (1993) *Children, Transport and the Quality of Life* London: Policy Studies Institute

Hornby, G. (2000) *Improving Parental Involvement* London: Cassell

Hughes, M. (1986) *Children and Number* Oxford: Blackwell

Hutt, S. J., Tyler, C., Hutt, C. and Christopherson, H. (1989) *Play Exploration and Learning* London: Routledge.

Illich, I. (1971) *Deschooling Society* Calder and Boyars Reprint, Harmondsworth: Penguin Education 1973

Jeffrey, B. and Woods, P. (2003) *The Creative School: A Framework for Success, Quality and Effectiveness* London: Routledge

Johnstone, R. (2004) Early Language Learning in Formal Education, in Byram, M. *Routledge Encyclopedia of Language Teaching and Learning* London: Routledge

Kane, P. (2004) *The Play Ethic* London: MacMillan

Katz, L.G. (1999) Another Look at What Young Children should be Learning *ERIC Digest* Available at: http://ceep.crc.uiuc.edu/eecearchive/digests/1999/katzle99.html (Accessed: 2 June 2006)

Kellert, S. and Wilson, E.O. (1984) *The Biophilia Hypothesis* Washington DC; Island Press

Kelly, A.V. (1999) *The Curriculum Theory and Practice* (4th Edition) London: Paul Chapman Publishing

Kenway, J., and Bullen, E. (2001) *Consuming Children* Buckingham: Open University Press

John-Steiner, V (2000) *Creative collaboration* London: Oxford.

Lancaster, Y. P. (2006) *RAMPS A Framework for Listening to Children* Daycare Trust London

Langer, E. (1997) *The Power of Mindful Learning* Reading, Cambridge MA: Addison-Wesley

Langston, A. (2006) Why Parents Matter, in Abbott, L. and Langston, A. (eds) *Parents Matter – Supporting the Birth to Three Matters Framework* Maidenhead: Open University Press

Living Streets (2005) Available at: http://www.livingstreets.org.uk/ (Accessed: 3 January 2006)

McCulloch, G. (2005) (ed) *The RoutledgeFalmer Reader in History of Education* London: RoutledgeFalmer

Malone, K. and Tranter, P. (2003) *Environmental Education Research* (9) 3

Marsh, J. and Millard, E. (2000) *Literacy and Popular Culture* London: Paul Chapman Publishing

Martin, F. and Owens, P. (2004) Young Children Making Sense of the World, in Scoffham, S. (ed) *Primary Geography Handbook* Sheffield: Geographical Association

Merttens, R. (1999) Family Numeracy, in Thompson, I. (ed) *Issues in Teaching Numeracy in Primary Schools* Buckingham: Open University Press

Millar, S. (1968) *The Psychology of Play* Harmondsworth: Penguin

Miller, L., Cable, C. and Devereux, J. (2005) *Developing Early Years Practice* London: David Fulton

Montague Smith, A. (1997) *Mathematics in Nursery Education* London: David Fulton

Nachmanovitch, S. (1990) *Free Play; Improvisation in Life and Art*, New York: Penguin Putnam

Newson, J. and E. (1979) *Toys and Playthings in Development and Remediation* London: George Allen and Unwin

Nunes, T. and Bryant, P. (1996) *Children Doing Mathematics* London: Blackwell

Nunes T., Schliemann A. L. and Caraher D. (1993) *Street Mathematics and School Mathematics* New York: CUP

OECD (2001) *Early Childhood Education and Care Policy in Denmark*, OECD Country Note Available at: http://www.oecd.org/edu/earlychildhood (Accessed: 2 June 2006)

Owens, P. (2004) Voices from an Inner City School: a Snapshot Study of Young Children's Learning in Outdoor Contexts, in Bowles, R. *Register of Research in Primary Geography: Play and Space* London: Register of Research in Primary Geography

Oxfam (2006) *Education for Global Citizenship: A Guide for Schools* GB: Oxfam

Oxfordshire Forest School Available at: http://www.oxfordshire.gov.uk/index/learning/schools/forestschools.html (Accessed 2 June 2006)

Pachler, N. and Field, K. (1999) *Learning to Teach Modern Foreign Languages in the Secondary School* London: Routledge

Paley, V.G. (1984) *Boys and Girls: Superheroes in the Doll Corner* Chicago: University of Chicago Press

Peacock, A. (2004) *Eco-literacy for Primary Schools* Stoke-on-Trent: Trentham Books

Pedersen, B. K. (2005) *Børn og motion* (Children and Exercise) Denmark, Nyt Nordisk Forlag

Pellegrini, A.D., Huberty, P.D. and Jones, I. (1995) The Effects of Recess Timing on Children's Playground and Classroom Behaviours *American Educational Research Journal* 32 pp645-64

Phenice, L.A. and Griffore, R.J. (2003) Young Children and the Natural World *Contemporary Issues in Early Childhood* 4 (2) pp167-171

Philpott, C. and Plummeridge, C. (2001) *Issues in Music Education* London: Routledge

Piaget, J. (1954) *Intelligence and Affectivity: Their Relationship During Child Development* Palo Alto, CA: Annual Review

Planning a Sensory Garden Available at: http://www.bbc.co.uk/gardening/gardening_with_children/plantstotry_sensory.shtml (Accessed: 1 August 2006)

Pound, L. (1999) *Supporting Mathematical Development in the Early Years* Buckingham: OUP

Radford, M. (2004) The Subject of Spirituality, in Hayes, D. (ed) *The RoutledgeFalmer Guide to Key Debates in Education* London: Routledge Falmer

Ribbens McCarthy, J. (2005) Negotiating Public and Private: maternal mediations of home-school boundaries, in Crozier, G. and Reay, D. *Activating Participation Parents and Teachers Working Towards Partnership* Stoke on Trent: Trentham

Richards, C. and Taylor, P.H. (eds) (1998) *How Shall we School Our Children? Primary Education and Its Future* London: Falmer Press

Risager, K. (2004) Cultural Awareness, in Byram, M. *Routledge Encyclopedia of Language Teaching and Learning* London: Routledge

Rogoff, B. (2003) *The Cultural Nature of Human Development* Oxford: Oxford University Press

Ross, N. (2004) Researching Children's Geographies using a Multi Method Approach, in Bowles, R. *Register of Research in Primary Geography: Play and Space* London: Register of Research in Primary Geography

Roth, W-M. (2003) Scientific literacy as an emergent feature of collective human praxis *Journal of Curriculum Studies* 35 (1) pp 9-23

Rushkoff, D. (1996) *Playing the Future* New York: Harper Collins

Seefeldt, C. (1999) (ed) *The Early Childhood Curriculum Current Findings in Theory and Practice* (3rd Edition) New York: Teachers College Press

Selter C (1999) How Old is the Captain? *Strategies* 5(1)

Shropshire Forest Schools Available at: http://www.shropshire.gov.uk/forestschools.nsf (Accessed: 2 June 2006)

Sibley, D. (1995) Families and Domestic Routines: Constructing the Boundaries of Childhood, in Pile, S. and Thrift, N. (eds) *Mapping the Subject: Geographies of Cultural Transformation* London: Routledge

Smith, A. (1998) *Accelerated Learning in Practice* Trowbridge: Redwood Books

Smith, A.B. (1993) Early Childhood Educare: Seeking a Theoretical Framework in Vygotsky's work *International Journal of Early Years Education* 1 (1) pp 47-61

Spencer, C. (2004) Place Attachment, Place Identity and the Development of the Child's Self Identity: Searching the Literature to Develop an Hypothesis, in Catling, S. and Martin, F. (eds) *Register of Research in Primary Geography: Researching Primary Geography* London: Register of Research in Primary Geography

Stephenson, A. (2003) Physical Risk-taking: dangerous or endangered? *Early Years* 23(1) pp35-43

TDA (2006) *Futures 2012* Available at: http://www.tda.gov.uk/partners/futures/general_interest_education.aspx (Accessed: 22 August 2006)

Theglander, B-L. (2001) *Folkeskolen* (The Folk-School Magazine) Number 37

Thompson, I. (ed) (1999) *Issues in Teaching Numeracy in Primary Schools* Buckingham: OUP

Thornton, L. and Brunton, P. (2005) *Understanding the Reggio Approach* London: David Fulton

Titman, W. (1994) *Special Places, Special People: The Hidden Curriculum of School Grounds* Godalming: World Wide Fund For Nature/Learning through Landscapes.

UNICEF *The Convention on Children's Rights* available at http://www.unicef.org/crc/index_30160.html (Accessed: 19 August 2006)

Vrdlovçova, J. (2005) Waking up to Waste *Primary Science Review* 86 pp 8-11

Vygotsky, L. (1978) *Mind in Society: The Development of Higher Psychological Processes* Cambridge MA: Harvard University Press

Walker, B.M., and MacLure, M. (2005) Home-School Partnerships in Practice, in Crozier, G. and Reay, D. *Activating Participation Parents and Teachers Working Towards Partnership* Stoke on Trent: Trentham

Walsh, D. (2005) Developmental Theory, in Yelland, N. *Critical Issues in Early Childhood Education* Open University Press

Waterfield, G. (ed) (2004) *Opening Doors: Learning in the Historic Environment* London: The Attingham Trust

Williams-Siegfredsen, J. (2005) Take the Risk *Nursery World* 4 August 2005

Wilson, R. (1999) Special Places for Young Children *Roots* 15 pp 26-30

Wood, E. and Attfield, J. (1996) *Play, Learning and the Early Childhood Curriculum* London: Paul Chapman Publishing

Woods, P. (1995) *Creative Teachers in Primary Schools* Buckingham: Open University Press

Worthington, M. and Carruthers, C. (2003) *Children's Mathematics: Making Marks Making Meaning* London: Paul Chapman Publishing

Wragg, E.C. (2004) *Education, Education, Education: The Best Bits of Ted Wragg* London: RoutldegeFalmer

Wyse, D. (ed) (2004) *Childhood Studies: an Introduction* Oxford: Blackwell Publishing

Index

angle 59-60

behaviour 1, 9, 65, 70, 79, 83, 88, 90
books and stories 4, 28, 30, 31, 78, 82, 122-123, 124, 132, 133-134
brain function 70-71, 88
buildings 27-29, 33-51, 57-58

calculations 53-54
challenge 66-67, 71, 81
citizenship 25, 31, 104, 119
cognitive development 64, 83, 88, 90, 104, 105
collaboration
    adults 14, 15, 69, 112, 116
    children 4, 9, 18, 48, 73, 90, 92
    children and adults 15, 25, 90, 114
commercialism 95, 98, 104
concentration 17, 69, 84, 88, 125
consumer education 98-104
co-operation 32, 64, 72, 73, 90, 100, 112
creative development 7, 10, 26, 80, 90, 93, 105, 116
creativity 11, 17, 50, 93, 95
cross-curricular 3, 34, 50, 80, 82, 92, 120, 125

culture 15-16, 18, 20, 34, 50, 64, 67, 82, 85-86, 94, 97 85, 97, 102-103, 108, 112, 120, 130
    popular culture 24, 95-105
curriculum 2, 10, 15, 17, 26, 55, 64-65, 76-77, 79, 80-84, 93, 119, 120, 129
Curriculum Guidance for the Foundation Stage 25, 33, 55, 92

dance 8, 91, 93, 94, 103, 132-133
dangers 24, 31, 66, 71, 130
design technology 99-104
diversity 30, 119, 120
dynamics 41-42

early learning goals 15, 92
emotional development 7, 8-9, 23, 64, 77, 79, 92-93, 120
engagement 9, 11, 22, 50, 54, 115
enquiry 26-27
exercise see physical activity
exploration 20-31, 33-34, 61, 63, 73, 76-77, 90, 96, 99, 119, 133

first hand experiences 17, 26, 30, 53-55, 66-69, 71, 122, 133

gardens 3, 4, 19, 27-28, 31, 57, 77, 91, 131
gender stereotyping 83, 98
global issues 117-120, 127, 132

happiness 17, 65, 71, 110
health 21, 69-70, 77, 88, 90, 103, 111, 129, 130

independence 9, 68, 76, 77
inquisitiveness 2, 9, 11, 25, 66, 96, 120

joy 65, 73, 86, 96

knowledge and understanding of the world 25, 80, 92

language development 9, 15, 64, 71, 73, 93, 120, 131
listening 32, 46, 65, 92, 105, 125
literacy 6, 64, 93, 95, 102, 105
local community 15, 25-26, 30, 56, 61, 118, 119, 126, 132
local environment 10, 23-32, 60, 93, 131-132

maps 5, 28, 60, 122

mathematical development 17, 53-61, 79, 93, 105
mud 17-18
multimedia resources 5, 6-8, 24, 28, 30, 46, 49, 54, 56, 57, 80, 95, 97, 99, 100, 103-105, 111, 114-115, 118 123, 124, 128
multisensory experiences 3-7, 19, 24-25, 65, 77, 86, 88, 90, 92
music 5, 8, 30, 33-51, 92,103, 123-124, 130, 132
musical structures 39-40

number lines 56-57

observation 6-7, 16, 26, 32, 66

parents 14, 22, 25, 67-68, 78-80, 101-103, 107-116, 121, 124, 125, 132
peace 7, 13, 19, 68, 73, 91
percussion 44, 49, 91
performing 50-51
physical activity 20-21, 24, 70, 85-91, 93
physical development 65, 66, 69-70, 77, 83, 87-88, 92
pitch 44-45

play 1-2, 14, 17-18, 23, 26, 63 65-66 69, 78, 82-83, 89, 90-92, 95-96 103
playground 17, 21, 24, 37, 41-43, 92, 111
pleasure 2, 20, 65, 71, 86, 112
practitioners' role 9, 10, 14, 15, 18, 21-22, 25, 50-51, 66, 71, 92
problem solving 54-55, 56, 59, 90, 96

questioning 4, 9, 26-29, 32, 51, 55, 57, 66, 129
recycling 20, 81, 99, 102, 130, 131-133
relationships 15, 27, 108, 109-116, 119
rich tasks 8-9
risks see also safety, danger 24, 66-67, 69 82
rondo 49
routines 65, 69, 124-125

safety 2, 14, 15, 20, 21, 24, 27, 32, 50, 65-67, 76, 81
school grounds 3, 8, 10, 15-16, 87
scientific development 17, 20, 95, 135
self esteem see also self image 10, 51, 65, 76, 79, 81, 133
shape 57-58

shops 53, 101-102
silence 46
social development 32, 69, 90, 92-93, 120
sound walk 4-5, 46
stories see books and stories
story telling 17-18, 103, 132

tempo 41
texture 42-43
timbre 35-38
tools 67, 76, 81-82

values 26, 64, 67-68, 97, 119
visits 30, 31

waste 31, 130-132
weather 20, 31, 48, 66, 76, 78, 91, 127, 129
well-being 15-17, 23, 25, 34, 70, 110
wonder 17, 19, 31, 65, 66
word problems 54-55